DECORATIVE PAINTING
SOURCEBOOK

DECORATIVE PAINTING
SOURCEBOOK

Edited by

Jennifer Long

Sandra Carpenter

Anne Hevener

NORTH LIGHT BOOKS

Cincinnati, Ohio

Decorative Painting Sourcebook. Copyright © 1997 by North Light Books. Manufactured in China. All rights reserved. No part of this book may be reproduced in any form or by any electronic or mechanical means including information storage and retrieval systems without permission in writing from the publisher, except by a reviewer, who may quote brief passages in a review. Published by North Light Books, an imprint of F&W Publications, Inc., 1507 Dana Avenue, Cincinnati, Ohio 45207. (800) 289-0963. First edition.

Other fine North Light Books are available from your local bookstore, art supply store or direct from the publisher.

01   00   99   98   97   6   5   4   3   2

Library of Congress Cataloging-in-Publication Data

    Decorative painting sourcebook / edited by Jennifer Long, Sandra Carpenter, Anne Hevener.
       p.   cm.
    Includes index.
    ISBN 0-89134-782-8 (alk. paper)
    1. Painting—Technique. 2. Decoration and ornament—Technique. I. Long, Jennifer. II. Carpenter, Sandra. III. Hevener, Anne.
NK2175.D4   1997
745.7′23—dc20   96-41200
                                   CIP

Edited by Jennifer Long and *Decorative Artist's Workbook* editors Sandra Carpenter and Anne Hevener
Production edited by Amy Jeynes
Interior designed by Clare Finney
Cover designed by Brian Roeth

The credits on page 122 constitute an extension of this copyright page.

North Light Books are available for sales promotions, premiums and fund-raising use. Special editions or book excerpts can also be created to specification. For details, contact: Special Sales Manager, F&W Publications, 1507 Dana Avenue, Cincinnati, Ohio 45207.

METRIC CONVERSION CHART		
TO CONVERT	**TO**	**MULTIPLY BY**
Inches	Centimeters	2.54
Centimeters	Inches	0.4
Feet	Centimeters	30.5
Centimeters	Feet	0.03
Yards	Meters	0.9
Meters	Yards	1.1
Sq. Inches	Sq. Centimeters	6.45
Sq. Centimeters	Sq. Inches	0.16
Sq. Feet	Sq. Meters	0.09
Sq. Meters	Sq. Feet	10.8
Sq. Yards	Sq. Meters	0.8
Sq. Meters	Sq. Yards	1.2
Pounds	Kilograms	0.45
Kilograms	Pounds	2.2
Ounces	Grams	28.4
Grams	Ounces	0.04

ACKNOWLEDGMENT

The editors of North Light Books and *Decorative Artist's Workbook* wish to thank the artists, photographers and contributors who generously allowed their work to be reprinted in this book.

ONTENTS

PART TWO: SUPPLIES AND RESOURCES

INTRODUCTION

Decorative painting is—like any other art form—an expression of creativity. With simply paint and a brush, a decorative painter can turn an ordinary object into a work of art. What's unique to this particular art form is its decoration of functional surfaces. Wooden boxes, shelves and furniture, tin trays and pitchers, linens and clothing, baskets, glassware—all these items (and many, many more) are fair game for painting. As many decorative painters will tell you—if it doesn't move, paint it!

Another feature that distinguishes decorative painting from many other art forms is that anyone with a desire to learn can become a decorative painter. Of course, to perfect your craft and develop your own individual style you'll need to practice, but a beginning painter can achieve beautiful results with only an introduction to the basic tools and techniques. Once you've experienced the joy of accomplishment and the therapeutic pleasure of painting, it's easy to understand why so many beginners fall in love with decorative painting for life.

The purpose of this *Sourcebook* is to provide you with an introduction to the basics of decorative painting—to demonstrate, step by step, everything you need to know to get started. And, even if you're not a beginner, you'll find a number of professional tips, resources and project ideas—as well as techniques you may not be familiar with—all here in one place, right at your fingertips.

The information, gathered from the pages of *Decorative Artist's Workbook* (a leading magazine in the field of decorative painting since 1987), includes instructions from many of the leading painters and teachers in the industry—Priscilla Hauser, Phillip Myer, Gretchen Cagle, Sherry Nelson and Jackie Shaw, to name a few. This bimonthly magazine is a continuous source of original patterns, step-by-step painting instructions, tips from the experts and new product information for decorative painters across the country and around the world.

The first part of the *Sourcebook* demonstrates basic brush strokes—the building blocks of beautiful designs. You'll also find tips for surface preparation and finishing, as well as step-by-step demonstrations of common blending, painting and *faux* finishing techniques. And, since decorative painting requires—in addition to a familiarity with the techniques—an assortment of tools and materials, the *Sourcebook* also includes a list of manufacturers and resources in its final pages.

While this book is first and foremost a reference book, it's also meant to be a source for inspiration. Once you've mastered the basics, do a little experimenting and make your own artistic discoveries.

Now, grab something that isn't moving and start painting!

PART ONE

TIPS AND TECHNIQUES

BASIC BRUSHSTROKES

Brushstrokes form the foundation of decorative painting. Just as the letters of the alphabet combine to form sentences, brushstrokes combine to form decorative designs. You can use them to create intricate scroll designs as well as all types of flowers and leaves. Once you master the following basic strokes—from the comma to the scroll—you'll paint faster, with more brush control, and finish your projects with more satisfying and consistent results.

The following basic strokes can be done with any of the basic brush types: a liner, round or flat brush. The only difference among these brushes is that you'll use the chisel edge of the flat brush, while you'll use the tip of the round or liner brush (see photo on the facing page). Brushes should be in good condition with no stray hairs. See page 99 in the Supplies and Resources section for a complete guide to brushes and the strokes best suited to each.

Both oil and acrylic paints should be mixed to a thin, creamy consistency so that they flow through the hairs of your brush smoothly, without being runny. Squeeze the paint onto a palette, then—if necessary—use a palette knife to work the paint to this consistency. Stroke the brush hairs through the puddle of paint until every hair is fully loaded, being careful not to load the tip so much that paint drips off.

Hold the brush loosely between your thumb and forefinger at the ferrule, and keep the handle straight up as you paint. When forming the strokes, balance the weight of your hand on your little finger, keeping your arm and wrist off the painting surface. Paint the strokes in one fluid motion.

You may find it helpful to lay tracing paper over these examples to practice making the strokes, or experiment on scrap paper. Grab your brush and let's get started!

Tip Stroke

Also called a chisel stroke if painted with a flat brush, this is one of the simplest decorative painting strokes. Like the name implies, the only part of the brush you'll use is the tip of a round or liner brush as shown at right, or the chisel edge of a flat brush. Even though the stroke looks like a thin, straight line, there's a definite technique to doing it right.

Step 1: Touch the tip of your brush to the surface, keeping the handle straight up.

Step 2: Using very little pressure, drag the brush toward you. The handle, however, should move away from you slightly as you paint. Take care to keep the stroke the same width from beginning to end. To finish, lift your brush cleanly off the surface.

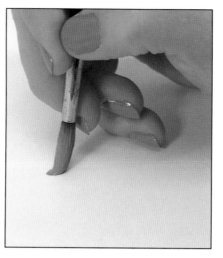

Step 1

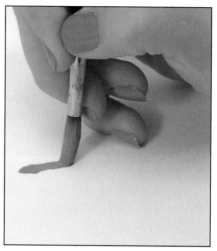

Step 2

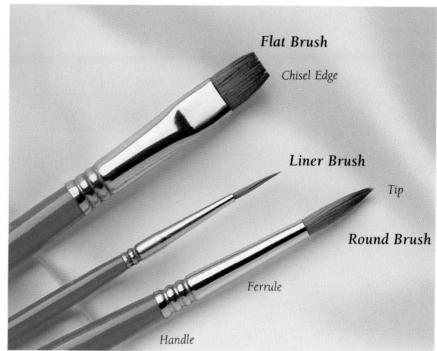

Flat Brush

Chisel Edge

Liner Brush

Tip

Round Brush

Ferrule

Handle

Broad Stroke

This stroke is very similar to the tip stroke, except that it's thicker. It's painted in the same manner regardless of the brush you use.

Step 1: Keeping the handle straight up, touch the surface with the tip of your brush. Apply gentle pressure so the hairs flatten out.

Step 2: Pull the brush toward you with light pressure. Your hand should move with the brush, so the handle will remain perpendicular to the surface instead of moving away from you as it did when you painted the tip stroke. Now, lift the brush up completely. The end of your stroke should be clean and crisp.

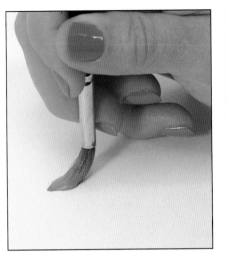

Step 1

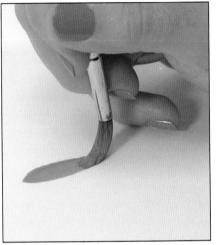

Step 2

Comma Stroke

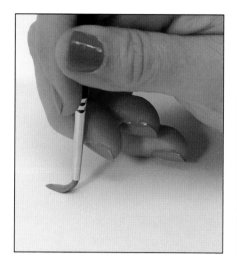

Step 1

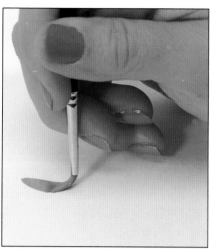

Step 2

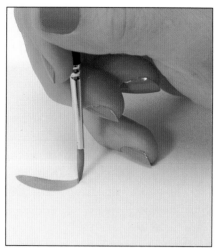

Step 3

One of the most recognizable strokes, the comma is also one of the most fun to paint. Commonly used in all forms of folk art and decorative painting, the comma stroke can be angled either to the left (as shown here), or to the right.

Step 1: Begin by pointing the tip of your brush hairs toward the left, holding the brush so the handle stands straight. Touch your brush to the surface and press it down gently so the brush hairs fan out to form a rounded head.

Step 2: Gradually lift the brush back up to its tip or chisel edge as you drag it forward, angling it slightly to the left (or right) as you lift. The handle should remain straight.

Step 3: Continue to release pressure until only the brush tip touches the surface. Then, lift the brush cleanly off the surface. Practice this stroke slowly until you've mastered the "touch, press, lift" motion. To stay in total control when completing this stroke, go through the following steps until they become second nature:

1. Slow down near the end of the stroke.
2. Let the hairs of the brush return to their natural configuration.
3. Stop, keeping the point (or chisel edge) of the brush still in contact with the painting surface.
4. Finally, and deliberately, lift up the brush.

Practicing these steps will eliminate ragged endings and comma strokes with multiple tails.

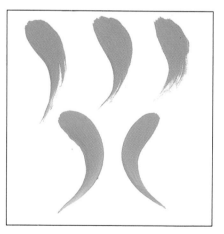

Ragged tails on your comma strokes (such as the top three) are frequently caused by stray brush hairs, a poorly loaded brush or a too-quick ending. With practice and the proper tools, you'll soon master proper strokes as perfect as the pair shown here.

Teardrop Stroke

The teardrop stroke looks a lot like the comma, but its head is at the bottom of the stroke rather than at the top. Also, there's more paint in the head of the teardrop stroke, so it doesn't look as smooth as the comma. Painters commonly use this stroke to embellish and add realism to painted flowers. This demonstration shows a straight teardrop, but you can also angle the stroke as in illustration below.

Step 1: To create the stroke, first load your brush so there's plenty of paint in the middle of the bristles. Next, twirl the bristles so they form a point. Hold the brush in an upright position and, using light pressure, begin creating the thin end of the stroke.

Step 2: Pull the brush toward you, gradually adding pressure to form the round head. Then, stop and lift the brush straight up. The brush handle should move away from you as you drag the tip forward to form the head.

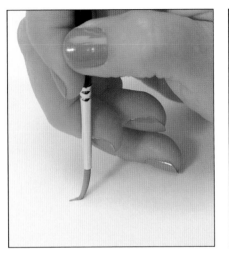

Step 1

Step 2

C-Stroke

Named after the letter it resembles, the C-stroke can be painted in a variety of ways. It can have sharp edges or look like smooth half-moons. Although the basic C-stroke is shown here, this stroke can also open toward the left to form a reverse C.

Step 1: Touch the tip or chisel edge of your brush to the surface, dragging it slightly to the left to create a thin, straight line.

Step 2: Now with the tip of the brush facing you, gradually apply gentle pressure on the brush so that the hairs fan out almost to the ferrule.

Step 3: Drag the brush toward you, lifting it slowly until only the tip or edge is touching the surface.

Step 4: Finally, drag the tip of the brush to the right to complete the C, as you slowly lift it off the surface. Notice that the handle of your brush will move slightly away from you as you press on the brush, but will only move upward as you lift and drag.

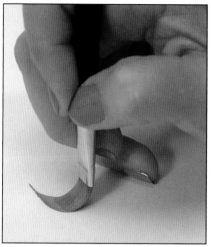

Step 1

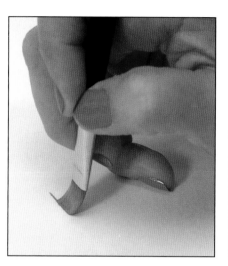

Step 2

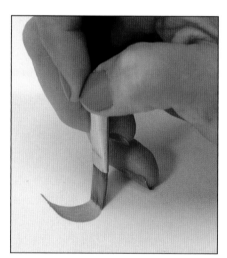

Step 3

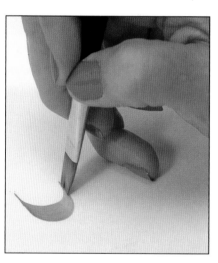

Step 4

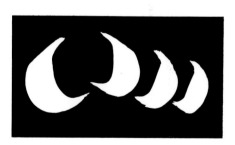

S-Stroke

To paint this elegant stroke, you have to be aware of the angle of your brush at all times. While you're painting the S, notice that the handle moves only slightly. It's the pressure on the hairs of the brush and the lifting back to the tip which form your stroke. The S-stroke is angled to the right—like the letter—in this demonstration but can also be angled to the left.

Step 1: Angle the tip or chisel edge of your brush toward the right corner of your surface, keeping the handle straight while you lightly paint a thin, downward line from one o'clock to eight o'clock.

Step 2: Now, gently change direction to form the middle section of the S, and drag your brush down toward five o'clock while gradually increasing the pressure so the hairs of the brush fan out.

Step 3: As you reach the center of the stroke, gradually release your pressure on the brush while continuing to pull. Now begin to gently lean the brush toward seven o'clock again as you slowly lift the brush back to the tip.

Step 4: Continue to drag the tip toward the left, lifting it off the surface to complete the stroke.

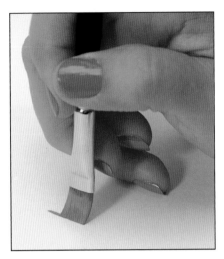

Step 1

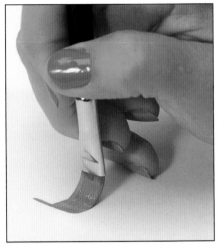

Step 2

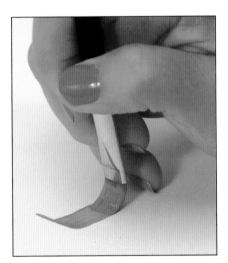

Step 3

Step 4

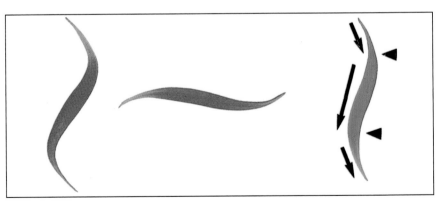

The S-stroke should be made in one smooth motion. Experiment with painting the S-stroke in different directions to find the one easiest for you. Apply gradual pressure before changing direction. Then, release pressure slowly before beginning a change in direction.

Crescent Stroke

This stroke looks like an upside-down U with slightly angled tips, so it's created by pulling the brush at an angle. Here the stroke has been painted with a flat brush so you can clearly see the change in the angle. (If you're left-handed, simply reverse these directions so that you move from right to left.)

Step 1: To begin, touch the chisel edge of your brush to the surface, keeping your brush handle perfectly straight. Now drag the flat edge of your brush away from you.

Step 2: Gradually apply pressure on the brush. When the hairs are nearly flat on the surface in the midsection of the stroke, swing the brush gently to the right. This is the widest part of your stroke.

Step 3: Now, slowly release the pressure on your brush until only the flat edge touches the surface.

Step 4: Drag the brush toward you until the line becomes thin. Stop and lift the brush cleanly off the surface to complete the stroke.

Step 1

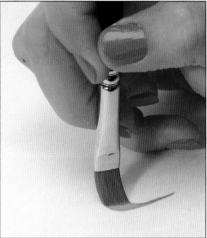

Step 2

Step 3

Step 4

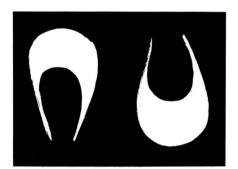

Scroll Stroke

The scroll stroke is actually a combination of the chisel and broad strokes, with an added flourish at the end. This graceful stroke works especially well for creating flowers.

Step 1: Begin by dragging the chisel edge of your brush upward.

Step 2: Now, gradually apply gentle pressure on the brush so the hairs are almost flat on the surface as you pull the brush to the right.

Step 3: To finish the stroke, continue to pull your brush around as shown in the photo. Gradually release the pressure until you come back up to the chisel edge, and then lift the brush cleanly off the surface. You should notice a slight "swirl" in the paint where you ended the stroke.

Step 1

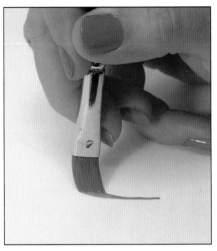

Step 2

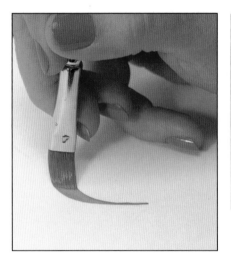

Step 3

Circle Stroke

Made with a flat brush, this stroke is handy for creating large, even circles for flower centers, grapes and cherries, and any other rounded design.

Step 1: Start with the chisel edge of your brush pointing toward three o'clock. Press down to fan out the brush hairs.

Step 2: Slowly pivot the handle and begin to drag the brush hairs toward six o'clock.

Step 3: Without lifting the brush, pivot the handle again, dragging the hairs toward nine o'clock.

Step 4: Complete the circle by pivoting the brush back to three o'clock, and then lifting the brush cleanly off the surface.

Step 1

Step 2

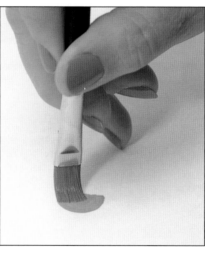

Step 3

Step 4

Dot Trick

The tip of your brush handle is your best tool for making perfectly shaped, uniform dots of all sizes. Just dip the rounded end of your brush into a puddle of paint and then gently press it onto your surface. The larger the handle and more paint you use, the larger the dot. Reload after each dot to maintain a uniform size, or print a series of dots without reloading to achieve a gradation from large to small dots.

𝒮TROKEWORK DESIGNS
Strokework Wooden Box

Once you've mastered the basic brushstrokes, you have the foundation for creating a variety of beautiful designs, from simple flowers to intricate motifs. Practice your skills by trying some of the projects and designs shown on the following pages. Simply copy the pattern to your surface using one of the transferring methods given on page 62. You can reduce or enlarge any of the patterns on a photocopier to adapt them to a smaller or larger surface.

Here you'll find complete instructions to take this strokework wooden box from start to finish, using a comma stroke as the basic design element. The painting process consists of five steps, as shown on pages 22-24.

Step 1: Sand your box, then wipe it clean with a tack cloth. Base coat the entire box with acrylic paint (teal was used in the example), applying several coats until you achieve opaque, even coverage. When the base coat is dry, apply a coat of water-based varnish with a sponge brush and allow it to dry.

Step 2: Transfer the pattern from page 25 onto the top of the box, enlarging or reducing if needed. Transfer the comma strokes and dot border from page 24 along the sides, using the photo on this page for placement.

This project has been divided from left to right to show the five steps necessary to complete this attractive box with a simple comma stroke design.

Base coat the design.

Paint the accents.

Step 3: Base coat the ball flowers with bright red. Base coat the tulip with a light blue. (A mixture of Titanium White, Ultramarine Blue and Mars Black was used on this project.) Base coat the blade leaves with green. Paint green comma stroke leaves on the top and sides of the box using a no. 4 round brush.

Step 4: Use the no. 4 round brush to paint comma strokes on the ball flowers. (In the example, Alizarin Crimson was used for the dark petals and Cadmium Orange for the lighter petals.) Paint light comma strokes on the tulip with white and dark comma strokes with a darker blue. (A mixture of Ultramarine Blue, Mars Black and a touch of white was used on the sample project.) Stroke over the leaves with light green, then with a medium yellow.

Step 5: Add trails of white dots using the tip of your brush handle. Don't reload the brush until you finish each row of dots. Use orange for the dots on the side borders, reloading frequently to keep the proportions equal. To add an antique finish to the box, prepare a glaze of Burnt Umber as shown on page 72. When the antiquing is dry, seal the project with several coats of a water-based varnish.

Antique the box.

Strokework Wooden Box Border Pattern

This pattern and the Wooden Box Lid Pattern on the next page can be reduced or enlarged on a photocopier to fit your surface. Use one of the transferring techniques described on page 62 to transfer the pattern to your project.

Wooden Box Lid Pattern

Strokework Tin

Turn a tin canister of any size into a tole treasure, perfect for homemade cookies and candies, as a housewarming gift, or for storing odds and ends. Apply your basic brushstroke skills to create this design in a snap.

Step 1: Choose a base color and spray paint the tin (green was used here). Allow to dry, then base coat the band using black acrylic paint and a sponge brush.

Step 2: Transfer the design on the following page to the sides and lid. (Enlarge or reduce the pattern on a photocopier if needed.) Paint the tulips using a dark, medium and light blue; the chrysanthemums are painted with a burgundy and bright red. Create the daisies with four circle strokes or the tip of a wide handle, using white and yellow paint. Make comma stroke leaves with a dark and medium green.

Step 3: Sponge a little black on either side of the black band. Create a border of comma strokes around the band. When dry, seal the tin with a clear acrylic spray. You can add an antiquing glaze using black oil paint thinned with turpentine over the sealer, if desired. When dry, finish with another coat of clear acrylic varnish.

Tin lid pattern.

Tin canister pattern.

©1992 PCM STUDIOS
Phillip C. Myer

Advanced Strokework Projects

Don't let the intricate designs fool you! You can create beautiful rosemaling-style projects like these with nothing but a little patience and the basic brushstrokes. Use the patterns provided and experiment with your own colors. Or, create your own unique designs using the brushstrokes you've learned.

Hanging heart.

Cracker tray.

Heart hook.

Heart key holder.

Cheese board.

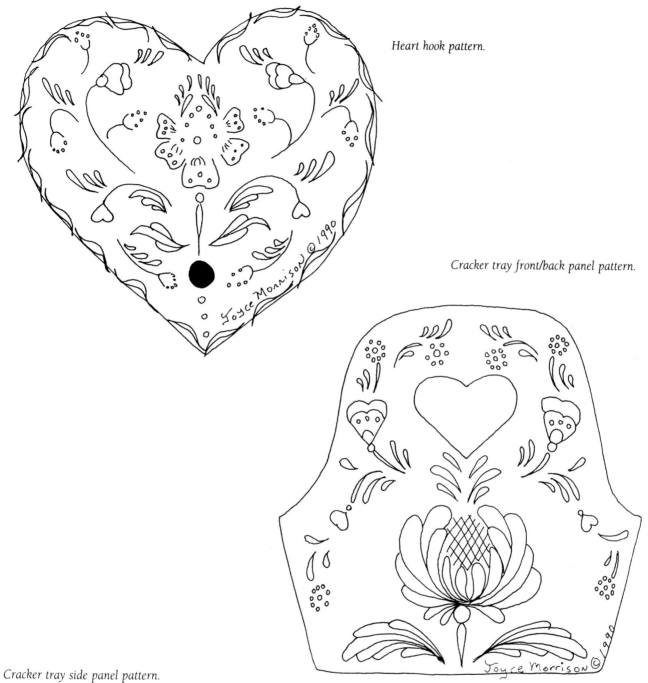

Heart hook pattern.

Cracker tray front/back panel pattern.

Cracker tray side panel pattern.

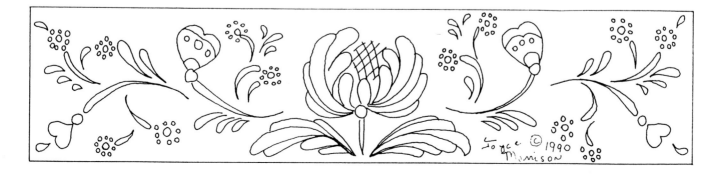

Cheese Board Pattern

Both sides of the cheese board pattern are identical, so simply trace one half, rotate the pattern, and trace the other side.

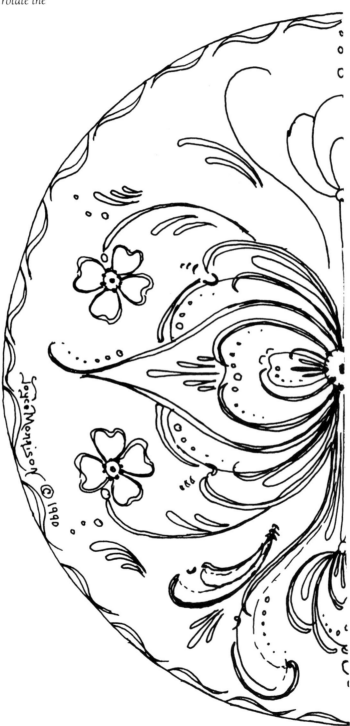

Hanging Heart Pattern

Heart Key Holder Pattern
*To make the key holder shown on page 28,
enlarge this pattern 133%.*

Creating Your Own Designs

Stroke Formations

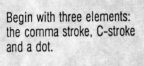

Begin with three elements: the comma stroke, C-stroke and a dot.

Put the elements together in any combination—there are no rules, just let your imagination run.

Add more comma strokes.

Change the size and position of the comma strokes and move the C-strokes.

Omit the C-strokes.

Use the C-strokes in a different way and face the large comma strokes outward.

Let the C-strokes overlap. Face the comma strokes inward.

Build a design by working from the outside in.

To create your own individual strokework designs, start by "doodling" with a medium-length liner brush. Your paint should be thinned to an ink-like, flowing consistency. After a little creative experimentation, you should have a few patterns which you can develop into full-blown designs. The decorative possibilities are endless when you combine and rearrange these basic elements. The following pages show a variety of design ideas and projects created with basic brushstrokes.

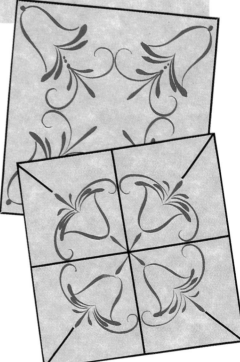

Experiment with the endless possibilities and see what other pleasing combinations you can create. Building your designs within a series of small boxes as shown will help you create a balanced motif.

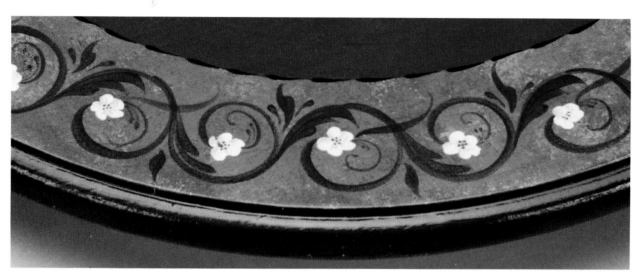

Scrolls, elongated comma strokes and clusters of dots form this fanciful floral border.

This step stool's intricate detail is entirely made up of basic brushstrokes. Teardrop strokes painted in a grid-like pattern form the side designs, while the comma, C-stroke and dot create the motifs and border on the top of each step.

Give your basic strokes an elegant appeal
with copper, gold or silver metallic paint.

Here a liner brush was used to draw delicate
scrolls, trace around comma strokes and
add brush-handle dots.

Simple comma strokes were used to create
this lacy border pattern.

A garden of strokework roses blooms on this
keepsake box.

Strokework is a quick way to give a large surface area, such as this stool, a highly detailed effect.

Both the border and the floral design on this plate were created with simple strokework.

Circle and comma stroke flowers adorn this antique album cover, lending a folk-art flavor.

SURFACE PREPARATION
Unfinished Wood

Trees can be divided into two categories—hardwoods and softwoods. Elegant hardwoods, such as cherry, walnut, oak and maple, are heavy and expensive, and often not available at art and craft stores. Pine, cedar and spruce are softwoods that are widely available and often used to create painting surfaces.

Prior to any decorative painting, a wood surface can be left *au naturel*; stained with a commercial stain or any color of oil or acrylic paint; or painted with opaque oil-based enamel or acrylic paint.

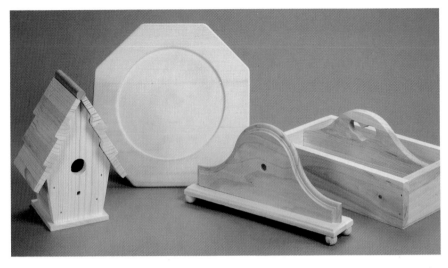

Craft and hobby stores carry a wide variety of unfinished wood surfaces just begging to be decorated. Look for birdhouses, sign boards, boxes, shelves, trays, clocks, wooden caddies and more.

STAINING WOOD

Step 1: Sand the surface with a fine-grade sandpaper or steel wool, and wipe it clean with a tack cloth.

Step 2: If you fear knots or undesirable marks will show through the stain over time, you may wish to seal the wood before you stain it. You can also seal the wood after you stain it, which will allow you to quickly wipe off any mistakes when adding decorative painting. However, paint adheres best to unsealed surfaces, so you may choose to hold off on the sealer until your project is complete. Opinions vary on sealing wood; it really comes down to experimentation and personal preference. When you apply sealer, firmly smooth the wood grain by sanding it with a piece of brown paper bag when your surface is dry.

Step 3: If using a commercial stain, carefully follow the directions on the label. If you choose to make your own stain, colors like Burnt Umber, Burnt Sienna and Raw Umber will give you a natural wood effect, while white and light pastel colors will create a washed effect called pickling.

If you're using oil colors, first brush the entire surface with turpentine (or try one of the new, safer turpentine substitutes) or linseed oil. This solvent will penetrate the raw wood, allowing the stain to flow smoothly and evenly.

Step 4: After wiping off excess solvent, mix one-fourth cup of the same solvent to approximately two inches of oil color in a wide-mouthed container. Apply the stain with either a sponge brush or soft rag, blending it into the grain and rubbing off excess. If you want a darker stain, add more oil color. If you want it lighter, use less oil color and more solvent. It's a good idea to experiment with your stain on a piece of inexpensive wood or an area that won't show before you begin staining your project. Let dry completely before adding decorative work.

Acrylic colors can be used in the same way as oils, substituting a product like Liquitex's Blending and Painting Medium for the oil solvent. Acrylic paints and water-based stains are safe, odor-free, and clean up with water, but they dry very quickly, which could leave dark splotches if you don't rub the stain into the grain immediately.

PAINTING WOOD

Step 1: First sand the surface smooth using fine grade sandpaper, and wipe it clean with a tack cloth.

Step 2: Brush on two or three coats of oil-based enamel or latex/acrylic paint. Flat, satin and gloss finishes all work well. Allow each coat to dry thoroughly before you apply the next; you may want to give the surface a light sanding between coats with a piece of plain brown paper bag. Sealing methods are the same as for staining wood.

Refinishing Wood and Wooden Furniture

These days, hand-painted, antiqued and personalized furniture is in demand. Rather than spending a fortune on new furniture, why not refinish old pieces? Revitalizing old wooden pieces isn't difficult; you don't need the skill of a master to get beautiful results.

Step 1: First determine what type of paint and/or varnish was originally applied to the piece so you can use compatible products for refinishing. Stick with all water-based or all oil-based products throughout the project; never intermix. Try these tests on a hidden area of the piece:

- If rubbing alcohol takes off the paint, it was probably an acrylic or latex product.
- If color comes off on a rag doused with turpentine, it was probably an oil/alkyd-based paint.
- Water-based varnishes are relatively new, so older furniture was probably finished with either oil/polyurethane varnish or lacquer/shellac.
- If the finish "gums" up or a yellowish tone shows on the rag when rubbed with turpentine, it is probably an oil-based varnish.
- If turpentine has no effect, but a lacquer/shellac thinner cuts through quickly, the finish is lacquer or shellac.

Step 2: If the piece is damaged or the finish is peeling, you'll need to repair these areas. Painting over flaws won't hide them; it will magnify them. Use wood putty and a putty knife to fill dents and cracks. For deeply recessed areas, build up layers as they dry and shrink until you achieve a level surface. Let dry, then sand smooth. You need to strip the surface only if it is covered with peeling or cracking paint or varnish.

Have the piece commercially stripped, or try one of the new, less toxic stripping products such as 3M's Safest Stripper.

Step 3: Once the piece is repaired, or if it is already in good shape, wash it with a solution of 40 percent water and 60 percent denatured alcohol. This will clean the surface and cut down on glossiness.

Step 4: Sand to create a tooth, or rough texture, for paint to adhere to, wiping clean with a tack cloth.

Step 5: Coat the wood with a good primer paint and/or sealer, remembering to use products compatible with the original finish. Your surface is now ready to be refinished, *faux* finished or painted with a decorative design. When the piece is dry, seal and protect it as you would do for raw wood.

Tin and Other Metals

Traditionally, the term "tole" painting specifically referred to painting on tin. (Today the term is sometimes used loosely to describe a style of painting, achievable on a number of surfaces.) But tin—be it an old piece or new—is still a popular choice for the decorative painter.

Step 1: Painting an old piece of tin or metal can give you a nice antique effect, but thorough cleaning and proper priming are essential to prevent peeling and flaking later on. If the piece is painted but existing paint is adhering well, simply clean it with dish detergent and water and dry the surface thoroughly before base coating with a new color. If, however, there is old paint on the piece that is chipping and peeling, you will need to use a good paint remover, carefully following the manufacturer's instructions. (Or, have the paint removed commercially.) Remove any rust with a commercial rust remover (found in most automotive stores), following the manufacturer's instructions carefully.

If you're starting with a new piece of tin or metal, wash it with dish detergent, then wipe it with white vinegar to remove any oils and dry thoroughly. Your piece is now ready to be primed with a rust-preventing metal primer and finished as described below.

Step 2: Prime the piece with a rust-preventing metal primer, the type used by auto body shops. (Your local auto body shop may be willing to spray your metal with primer for a small fee.)

This 50-year-old tin plate, painted by Robert Berger in folk-art style, is a favorite in Priscilla Hauser's personal collection. Other good metal projects include pitchers, lamps, trays and mailboxes.

Step 3: In most cases, the primer color works fine as a base coat; if not, apply another color over it. Spray-painting the base coat will give you a smoother, more even coverage than brush painting. It's important to check if the primer is oil- or acrylic-based, so you can choose a compatible paint. Let the piece dry and cure thoroughly.

Step 4: Now you're ready to trace your design onto tracing paper and transfer it to your surface.

Ceramic

Also known as earthenware, ceramic pieces come in a wide variety of shapes and forms, making them a wonderful surface for the decorative painter. A ceramic surface is made from a nonmetallic inorganic material, such as clay, and hardened by firing with heat. To achieve the best painting results, follow these tips for proper preparation of ceramic surfaces—both glazed and unglazed.

The milk-can-shaped canister shown here was found at a ceramics shop in the form of "greenware," meaning it was unfired. For a reasonable fee, the shop cleaned and fired the piece. After firing, the ceramic is called "bisque." Before applying any paint, bisque should be sealed, base coated lightly and sealed again. A piece of ceramic that has a satin or high gloss finish can also be painted, but it must be handled carefully as it's easily scratched. Ceramic pieces should never be put in the dishwasher; hand-wash or dust only.

Step 1: Wash the surface thoroughly.

Step 2: Seal the ceramic with a good all-purpose sealer, such as Jo Sonja's All Purpose Sealer or Krylon matte sealer.

Step 3: Spray or brush on the base coat color of your choice.

Step 4: Seal the base coat again lightly. Let dry, then begin your decorative painting.

Step 5: When the paint is completely dry, seal the ceramic with the acrylic sealer or varnish of your choice.

This apple canister is one of many wonderful ceramic shapes available to the decorative painter. Other popular ceramics include trinket boxes, vases, pitchers and figurines.

Glass

Although oil paint adheres to glass, quite well and doesn't need any type of primer, if you've ever tried using acrylic paint on glass, you know that it tends to slip around and does not stick easily. Don't give up! It can be done, and with less difficulty than you think. The secret to painting on glass lies in the preparation.

Step 1: Clean the glass thoroughly with alcohol, vinegar or ammonia. Be sure that any residues on the glass are removed, then allow to dry.

Step 2: Apply a base coat primer—a product that enables you to paint on top of the glass without the paint sliding around. Place the glass on top of your chosen design, then carefully apply the primer to the areas you'll be painting. To prime the glass, you can use:

1. An acrylic matte medium, which looks like white glue and is available in both matte and gloss finishes.
2. Jo Sonja's All Purpose Sealer.
3. An etching solution such as B&B Etching Cream.
4. A clear acrylic spray. Unless you want the entire surface to have a frosted look, this product will require masking off the areas you don't intend to paint, such as a background. Using a stencil card the size of the glass, cut out a sten-

A painting done on a flat piece of glass makes a unique, dimensional picture when mounted on burlap. Try painting flowers on an ordinary glass vase, or decorate jam jars filled with your homemade preserves to give as gifts.

cil of the areas you will be painting. Place it on the glass and spray the design area with acrylic spray. Let the base coat primer dry completely

Step 3: To transfer your pattern, neatly trace it onto tracing paper. You might want to do this with a fine line marking pen or permanent marker. Tape this to the back of your piece of glass. Then paint on top of the glass, following the pattern lines beneath.

Step 4: If you wish to varnish the design to protect it, apply the varnish to the painted area only.

Clay Pots

Terra-cotta flowerpots are an inexpensive, quick, easily accessible surface for decorative painting. Plant a collection of them on a windowsill, fill them with potpourri or give them as gifts.

Step 1: Scrub the pots with soap and water and let them dry thoroughly.

Step 2: Using acrylic paints, base coat the outside of the pot and the inside rim. Leave the rest of the inside unpainted.

Step 3: When the base coat has dried, you're ready to paint your design. Use your imagination; try plaid, flowers, geometric designs, stars and stripes or a *faux* finish. A sea sponge is ideal for sponging on color, and a small square of foam works well with stencils.

Step 4: Finish the pot with several light coats of a water-based varnish. Your flower pots are safe for outdoor use, but take them inside in the winter; terra-cotta will crack if left to freeze and thaw.

Clay pots can be painted to fit with any color theme or decor. Use stencils, metallic paints or your favorite faux finishing technique to turn plain pots into works of art.

Tiles

Painted tiles make an elegant accent for the kitchen or bath. Use them as trivets or coasters to dress up the dinner table and protect wood surfaces, or mount them on the wall as a border or splashback for everyone to admire. Colorful floral, fruit and vegetable motifs are perfect for the kitchen; or recreate the look of expensive Italian or Spanish painted tiles for any room in your home.

Step 1: Start with a finished (glazed) ceramic tile, available at ceramic studios, hardware and home improvement stores or anywhere flooring materials are sold. When buying tiles, it's worthwhile to ask for any broken tile pieces they have on hand. Use these to practice on, since painting on a slick surface can be tricky. It's a good idea to experiment with colors, too.

These purple pansy tiles work well as a trivet for hot dishes while adding a pretty touch to your dinner table.

Step 2: Use acrylic enamel paints, such as DecoArt Gloss Acrylic Enamels, which are designed for painting on hard, slick surfaces. As these paints don't become permanent until they are baked and cured, you can simply scrub off any mistakes. When the painting is complete, allow it to cure for twenty-four hours, then bake the tiles in a conventional oven at 325° for thirty minutes. Allow the tiles to cool in the oven before you remove them. Baking and cooling the tiles in this way sets the paint, making it relatively durable and dishwasher-safe. (NOTE: It's important to read and follow the instructions on the paint label carefully for best results. This paint is not considered food-safe. Be sure you don't use painted tiles for food preparation; and don't use this paint on any surface that comes in contact with food.)

Plaster

Plaster comes in a wide variety of forms, from tiny cherub moldings to weighty Greek pedestals. Because plaster is so porous, it requires a little more preparation work than some other surfaces, but the results will justify the effort. Imagine the impact of a *faux* marble pedestal graced with trailing potted ivy. Or, picture your holiday mantelpiece decked with a unique collection of painted Santas.

Step 1: If your plaster is damaged or uneven, fill in any recessed areas with a plaster patch, then sand with both medium- and fine-grade sandpapers. Take special care when cleaning your surface after sanding, being sure to wipe all the crevices with a tack cloth. Plaster surfaces are covered with dust.

Step 2: Prime the plaster with gesso using a soft, synthetic bristle brush. Since plaster is extremely porous, you'll need to apply at least three coats of gesso before the seal begins to form. Without the gesso, your paint will bleed into the plaster. On detailed pieces, you'll need to use a small brush to cover the recessed areas of the mold with gesso.

Step 3: Be sure to let each coat of gesso dry at least one hour, then sand the plaster lightly and wipe it with a tack cloth before applying another coat.

Step 4: Once the plaster is primed, lightly mist the surface with several coats of clear acrylic spray. Let dry, then base coat the plaster. Seal the base coat with acrylic spray and let dry before completing your painting.

Due to its porous nature, plaster must be primed and sealed before it can be painted.

Fabric

You can use literally any kind of paint on almost any fabric. Oils, acrylics, alkyds, watercolors, fabric paints and fabric dyes all work well for fabric painting. What type of paint you choose will depend on the effect you want, the type of fabric you use, how you'll use the fabric, and your washing preference for it. Keep the following characteristics in mind when choosing a medium for your fabric painting:

OIL COLORS

- Oils are ideal for elaborately blended designs that will take a long time to complete.
- They can be used on most fabrics except for silks and polyesters which don't "hold" paint as well.
- They will hold up through at least twenty washings before the color begins to fade.

ACRYLICS

- Acrylics can be used on all fabrics.
- They offer vibrant hues.
- They have a quick drying time (which also means you have less time for blending).
- They saturate fabric easily.
- They stay colorfast through multiple washings.

ALKYDS

- Alkyds have a longer "open time" than acrylics, giving you the blending capabilities of oils but with a faster drying time.
- Alkyds can be used on most fabrics with the exception of silk, polyester and polyester blends.

- They will hold their color about as well as oils.

WATERCOLORS

- Watercolors are good for "temporary" items; they are not permanent on fabric.
- They create a soft, washed look unlike any other medium.
- They can only be applied successfully to a few fabrics, such as 100 percent cotton.
- They can't be heat set or washed.

FABRIC PAINTS

- Fabric paints are designed solely for use on fabric. They are made of artist's powder pigment, binders, setting agents and chemicals for permanency.
- They work well on a variety of materials.
- They can be opaque, semitransparent or transparent.
- Most have enough "open time" for blending depending on the manufacturer.
- Intense colors will hold up well through repeated washings.

FABRIC DYES

- The only truly permanent medium, their intense hues saturate every fiber in the fabric, becoming stable and durable.
- They can be tricky to work with for the beginning painter as they're more difficult to tone down and control due to their ink-like consistency.
- They are ideal for all types of fabric with the exception of polyester and

fabrics with a high synthetic content.

Step 1: Wash your fabric before painting to avoid shrinking it later. Washing will also get rid of any chemicals or sizing in the fabric which might keep the paint from adhering to the fibers. Avoid using fabric softeners when washing the fabric, as they may prevent the paint from adhering properly.

Step 2: Transfer your design to the fabric using chalk transfer, a transfer pen or graphite paper, or draw it directly on the fabric.

Step 3: Tape a layer of plastic wrap to a piece of cardboard slightly smaller than the item you're painting; this will keep the paint from sticking to the cardboard. Cover the board with a layer of paper towels to absorb excess paint, and slip it directly under the fabric layer you're painting on. For instance, if you're painting the front of a sweatshirt, slip the cardboard inside the shirt.

Step 4: For heavily textured fabrics, it's best to use a "hog hair" or stiff nylon brush to scrub your base coat color into the fabric. Brushes specifically designed for fabric painting will last longer than regular artist's brushes as they've been specially designed to apply color to textured surfaces. Softer synthetic brushes are ideal for blending and base coating on smooth fabrics, while high-grade synthetic brushes are needed for fabric dyes as their bristles can hold plenty of color. Natural hair brushes won't hold up to the rigors of most fabric painting.

This beautiful spring bouquet was painted on silk using four basic colors of silk dye and a resist medium.

Step 5: Oil and alkyd colors should be thinned with a product such as Grumbacher's Textile Painting Medium. Thinning will also help speed up the drying time of oils. For acrylic painting, it's best to use a combination of water and acrylic textile medium. The textile medium will bond the paint to the fabric and will make the paint easier to apply. Your paint should be thinned to a creamy consistency so it flows smoothly. If the fabric is especially thick or textured, you may need to thin the paint more. If the paint "drags" across the fabric and is difficult to work in, you'll need to thin it to the consistency of ketchup.

Step 6: Use fabric marking pens for creating details where a liner brush would be difficult to use. Don't press hard, or your line will bleed.

Step 7: To finish, heat set the design to ensure the painted colors will stay permanent through washing. To heat set a design completed in acrylics or fabric paints, turn an iron to medium setting (do not use steam), place a sheet of typing paper or a pressing cloth over the painted area and press for a few minutes. You can also heat set your paint by ironing over the back of the design. To heat set a design done in oils or alkyds, use a pressing cloth soaked in vinegar. Fabric dyes don't need to be set. Items which can't be ironed can be heat set using a hairdryer.

Step 8: Turn washable items inside out when laundering. Delicate items should be hand-washed. Nonwashable items can be wiped with a damp sponge to remove dust and dirt.

Accidents

Since it's almost impossible to remove accidental paint splatters from fabric, try to create a new design element to incorporate the spot into your design. Trying to rub the spot off will only make it larger. If you get too much paint within your design area, simply pick up the excess with a damp brush. When using silk dyes, you can clean a spill by rubbing an alcohol-dipped brush against the splotch.

Papier-Mâché

Papier-mâché, which is French for "chewed (or pulped) paper," is a modeling material made from pulp or paper, water and a binding agent such as glue. Papier-mâché was first used in Europe in the eighteenth century, although it was probably used in the Far East long before then.

Papier-mâché is a hard, inexpensive, durable surface that wears well. In fact, it's actually more durable than wood, because unlike wood, it won't crack, expand, contract or warp when exposed to temperature changes. It also won't break easily when dropped.

Pre-made papier-mâché pieces can be found at most craft stores. Shapes include gourds; cones; boxes of various sizes and shapes such as squares, hearts and stars; and seasonal shapes such as reindeer, eggs, Christmas trees and pumpkins. Papier-mâché is one of the easiest surfaces to prepare and finish.

Step 1: Apply two or three base coats of oil or acrylic paint with a sponge brush. Let dry, then add your decorative painting.

Step 2: To finish, apply two or three coats of either water-based or spray-on varnish.

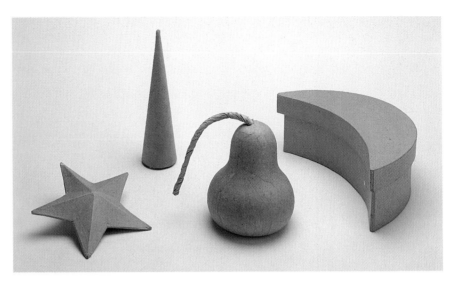

Papier-mâché comes in a wide variety of forms, including stars, cones, gourds and stackable boxes.

Homemade Papier-Mâché

To make your own papier-mâché objects, you can use this recipe:

- 4 cups shredded or torn-up paper, such as newspaper
- 1 cup water
- ½ cup dry wallpaper paste

Mix to form a solid mass, then shape as desired. When the piece is completely dry, sand it until it's smooth.

Another method calls for strips of paper and the following mixture:

- ¾ cup flour
- 2 cups water
- (or equal parts white glue and water)

Cut paper into long strips and dip in the glue mixture, then place on the desired surface. When dry, sand and paint.

For round shapes, try inflating a balloon to the desired size, then covering it with papier-mâché. Leave a small hole at one end where the tied end of the balloon protrudes. When thoroughly dry, pop the balloon and remove it through the hole, then cover the opening with a few more strips of paper.

Paper

In most cases, paper needs no surface preparation before painting. The exception is watercolor paper, which some artists prefer to wet or stretch before use. The real trick to painting on paper is understanding the terms used to describe different papers and knowing which is right for your project.

Tooth, or texture, is the most important characteristic to consider when choosing a paper. The terms *hot-pressed*, *cold-pressed* and *rough* refer to paper's tooth.

Hot-pressed papers have the smallest degree of tooth and are, therefore, the smoothest papers. They're great to use for pen-and-ink work and for drawing. The surface is created by running the paper between a series of rollers designed to even the texture for a smooth finish. A hot-pressed surface can be made smoother still by coating the surface with clay or plastic to make a *plate* surface that's ideal for ink work.

Cold-pressed papers haven't been pressed to the degree that hot-pressed papers have. The cold-pressed surface has a fair amount of tooth and is good to use for pencil and charcoal drawings. Cold-pressed papers are referred to by many different terms, including *vellum* and a *not* surface (as in *not pressed*).

Rough papers are similar to cold-pressed papers, only with a greater degree of tooth. The rough surface is normally used only in the production of watercolor papers. Rough papers add a great deal of unusual and individual character to colors, shapes and lines.

Sizing is another term you might see when picking out watercolor pa-

Shown from left to right are rough, cold-pressed and hot-pressed papers.

per. It refers to a gelatin coating applied to watercolor paper to control its absorbency. If sizing is added in the vat when the pulp is prepared, it's called *internal sizing*. If it's added to the surface of an already formed sheet, it's called *tub* or *surface* sizing. Tub-sized papers work well with watercolors because the sizing sits on the surface of the paper and keeps the paint from bleeding through the fibers.

WETTING YOUR PAPER

The most popular way to saturate the whole paper is to soak it in a tub of lukewarm water. If you plan to paint on saturated paper, when you remove it from the water, place it on a waterproof board to prevent the water from soaking into a porous material. Or, try one of these methods:

- Work on a Formica countertop in your kitchen or bath.
- Use a piece of ordinary glass or Plexiglas under your paper.
- Place your paper on top of a stack of pre-soaked newspaper to maintain a moist condition.

STRETCHING YOUR PAPER

When painting on thin, saturated paper, use either of these procedures to prevent or minimize buckling:

- Paper expands when wet, so staple all the edges to a wooden board while the paper is wet. Because it can't shrink, it will dry tight.
- Stretch the wet paper by sticking the paper's edges to a surface with nylon-reinforced brown packing tape (masking tape does not adhere to a wet surface). The glue of the tape is water soluble, sticks well to wet paper and is strong enough to prevent shrinkage.

Some manufacturers combine the advantages of heavy and thin papers by mounting thin paper on a heavy board. The hard surface won't buckle when wet, and it retains as much of a color's value as if you were using a stretched thin paper. If the board and the adhesive are acid-free, the paper will be archival quality and will never change color.

Baskets

Painting on the rough, uneven surface of a basket may sound tricky. The shape of the weave and the open spaces can make transferring a pattern challenging, but with a little experimentation, you'll achieve delightful results. When painting on baskets, it's important to stand back and study your painting every now and then. The effect is entirely different from a distance than it is when you're seeing it up close.

Step 1: If you're painting on a basket that isn't already painted or varnished, no surface preparation is needed. However, if your basket is painted with a gloss enamel finish, such as a white wicker basket, you'll need to create some tooth. Either sand the basket lightly or spray it lightly with an acrylic matte spray.

Step 2: Neatly trace your design onto a sheet of tracing paper. Turn the traced design facedown and firmly go over the lines with chalk. Shake off any excess dust and tape the pattern to the basket, chalk side down. Using a stylus or pencil, trace the lines again, transferring the chalk to the basket surface. The tracing process may be difficult due to the textured weave.

If you're having trouble and the design looks distorted, use a stylus or large pin to punch holes along the lines of the pattern. Tape the design in place on the basket and then rub chalk or white paint over the holes. When you remove the tracing paper, the dots will have transferred the design to the basket.

This charming country basket would be perfect for an old-fashioned fried chicken picnic.

Step 3: When painting, use a dabbing, pressing motion so the paint thoroughly coats the basket's weave. Base coating is necessary only if you want to create opaque coverage. To do so, use a small piece of sponge and thick acrylic paint and carefully dab and press the undercoat onto the basket. Let the base coat dry before painting your design.

Step 4: Coat the basket with the spray varnish of your choice. For a finishing touch, line your basket with fabric and paint a simple design around the rim.

Candles

Softly glowing painted candles make a lovely centerpiece for romantic dinners and seasonal festivities. Why not decorate a rose-scented candle with a floral design, or bright red and green candles with holiday motifs? Just remember, if you intend to burn the candle, don't spend hours painting a masterpiece on it, as it will eventually melt away! In this case a simple design is most effective.

Step 1: Painting on candles is very simple, but you must prepare the surface with a matte acrylic spray first. After you've sprayed the candle, don't touch the surface until it's completely dry, as the acrylic will soften the finish on the candle.

Step 2: You can use either oils or acrylics to paint on candles. Oils are a bit easier to use since you don't have to underpaint with them as with acrylics, and they adhere better to a candle since the candle itself is a bit oily. If you use oils, don't thin them down with any medium or turpentine, and use the paint sparingly.

If you use acrylics, you'll probably find that the first coat of paint will bead up or separate. Brush on your first coat of paint and let it dry. When you go back to paint a second coat, it will adhere quite nicely.

Step 3: When your finished painting is dry, be sure to coat the candle again with acrylic spray.

A collection of candles painted with holly leaves and berries adds a seasonal glow to any table or mantelpiece.

Gourds

Gourds are great surfaces to paint because of their unique shape and nice "tooth." Gourds are allowed to dry in the sun for about six months until they become hollow and very hard. When the outer skin peels, molds or turns white, the gourd is dry. This rough skin must be removed to get to the hard, paintable surface of the gourd.

Step 1: To remove the skin, immerse the gourd in very hot water for a few minutes, then enclose it immediately in a trash bag, trapping steam in the bag. After the gourd has steamed for an hour or two, scrub it with kitchen cleanser and a non-metal scouring pad to remove the softened skin. Let the gourd dry before painting it, and sand away any spots that didn't come off by scrubbing.

Step 2: After removing the skin, the gourd may still have some cracks, indentations or holes. To create a smoother painting surface, sand these imperfections with a fine-grade sandpaper and fill them with wood filler. Before painting the gourd, wipe it thoroughly with a tack cloth to remove any dust particles.

Step 3: You can paint on a gourd with almost anything; acrylic paints are commonly used, but oils and even opaque watercolors also work well. Watercolors result in softer colors and resemble the look of natural dyes. Whatever the medium, when the painting is dry, finish it with clear acrylic varnish.

For more information on gourds, contact the American Gourd Society, Inc., P.O. Box 274, Mount Gilead, OH 43338.

Painted gourds are the perfect accent for seasonal festivities. These Thanksgiving-themed gourds would look great as a centerpiece or perched atop a hay bale outside. Smaller gourds, like the Santas below, can be used as tree trimmings.

Pumpkins

Painting your Halloween pumpkins will not only make them look great, they'll also last much longer than carved ones. Plus, you won't have to clean up gooey orange hands, clothes or kitchen floors. And there will be no mushy remains to dispose of after Halloween!

Step 1: Wash your pumpkin thoroughly and let it warm up to room temperature (it's hard to get paint to adhere to a cold surface).

Step 2: You don't need to seal the pumpkin before you paint it, but if you prefer to, use an acrylic spray.

Step 3: You can transfer the pattern to the pumpkin using graphite or chalked paper, but it may be easier to freehand the design directly onto the pumpkin, using the pattern as a guide.

Step 4: You can use both oils and acrylics to paint your pumpkin, but since acrylics dry faster, they may be easier to use. Some creative options include painting the pumpkins white to make ghosts or black to create cats.

Step 5: Once you've painted the design, spray the pumpkin with several coats of a gloss spray varnish.

Step 6: Add the embellishments of your choice. The pumpkins shown here have painted wooden knobs for noses, hot-glued to wooden toothpicks which are pushed into the pumpkin. Use raffia ribbon to create wild hair, and crepe paper or bendable ribbon to fashion a hatband for witches' hats.

A little paint and a few accessories was all it took to turn ordinary pumpkins into these whimsical witches.

Side Loading

Side loading your brush is a fast, effective way to shade and highlight when you're working with oils or acrylics. To "side load" means to carry paint on one side of the brush and a medium on the other. Water is the most common acrylic medium; for oils, you'd use turpentine. A flat brush is normally used for side loading because its shape is ideal for loading both sides. However, a round brush can also be used. These directions are given using acrylic paint and water.

Step 1

Step 2

Step 3

Step 4

Step 1: Dip your brush in water.

Step 2: Blot the excess water on a paper towel.

Step 3: Stroke only one side of the brush through a puddle of paint; the water on that side will become saturated with color. On a clean area of your palette, gently stroke the brush back and forth to force the paint and water to blend together.

Step 4: A successfully side-loaded brush will produce a graduated tone when stroked on your painting surface. The stroke will be dark on one side, a medium tone in the center, and colorless on the opposite side.

Double-Loading

Double-loading your brush enables you to apply two colors at once and cuts down on the amount of blending you have to do. To "double-load" means to carry two colors side by side on the brush, with the colors blending together in the center. As in side loading, a flat brush is normally used. To double-load a brush, follow these simple steps:

Step 1: Begin by stroking one side of a brush through the edge of a puddle of paint (always load the lighter of the two colors first). Stroke against the edge of the color several times so the hairs of the brush become saturated with paint.

Step 2: Stroke the other side of the brush through the darker color. Again, be sure to saturate the hairs of the brush.

Step 3: On a clean area of your palette, pull the brush back and forth using very short strokes to force the paint through the hairs of the brush.

Step 4: Turn the brush over and stroke with the same short pulls. The colors are blending together in the center of the brush to provide a smooth transition of color. You may need to reload at this point to get enough paint in the brush. A successfully double-loaded brush, when stroked on your surface, will have a soft blend of two colors, one color on each side, which blend in the middle.

Step 1

Step 2

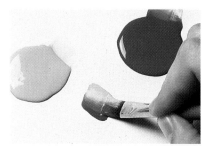

Step 3

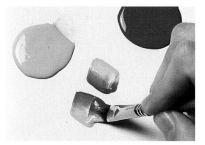

Step 4

Common Double-Loading Mistakes

If your brush runs out of paint quickly when you double-load it, look for and correct these common mistakes:

1. Your paint isn't thin enough to allow the hairs of the brush to receive it properly. The paint should be very thin and creamy.
2. Your brush isn't completely loaded with paint. Keep in mind that the bristles should have paint on them all the way up to the metal ferrule. (As long as you clean the brush properly when finished, this won't damage the hairs.) Practice stroking your brush through each color ten to twenty times. However, don't press down too hard as you can actually force paint out of the brush hairs.
3. You didn't form a "loading zone" on your palette. It's extremely important to blend in one spot on the palette, working first on one side of the brush and then on the other, to make sure the bristles are completely loaded with paint. Be careful not to flip your brush the wrong way; you don't want to mix your colors together.

Floating Color

Once you've mastered the technique of floating color, you'll find yourself using it anywhere you want a delicate transition from no color to subtle color. If you're painting with acrylics, you'll use water or a painting medium to float color, and if you're painting with oils or alkyds, you'll use turpentine. These directions are given using acrylics and water.

Step 1: Dip a flat brush into clean water and blot the excess on a paper towel.

Step 2: Dip a corner of the brush into a puddle of paint, and stroke it back and forth on your palette. The paint should spread to only half the brush. If the entire brush becomes filled with paint, clean it in water and start over. If the paint seems dry and "pulls" on the palette, the brush doesn't have enough water in it. Again, clean it well and start the process over.

Step 3: Place the paint-filled side of the brush where you want the darkest color, and using a smooth, gliding stroke, float the color on.

Step 4: The paint should glide onto the surface smoothly, blending evenly from dark to light with each stroke.

Step 1

Step 2

Step 3

Step 4

Dry Brushing

This technique, as the name implies, is accomplished with only a scant amount of paint in your brush. It is especially useful for building highlights or shading in your painting. Because it is hard on brushes, it's best to use an old, worn-out flat brush for this technique.

Step 1: Pick up a color with your dry brush using a color slightly lighter than your base coat if you are creating highlights or slightly darker if shading. Don't mix your paint with water or any medium.

Step 2: Wipe the brush on a paper towel to remove excess paint; you only need a touch of paint in your brush. Having too much will leave globs on the surface.

Step 3: Begin brushing the color on, scrubbing as if you were using a pencil eraser. Wipe off your brush often to assure that it remains dry. If you are creating a highlight use closely related colors as you build up multiple layers so that each layer is only slightly lighter than the last—don't jump to a much lighter value. Each layer should also occupy less space than the last, shrinking to the size of your final, strongest highlight. If you are shading, the process is reversed, building layers that are each slightly darker than the last. There should be no visible start or stop lines within your highlight or shadow.

The highlights on these grapes and roses were created using the dry-brush technique. Notice how the lighter areas of color gradually shrink into the brightest point of highlight.

Stroke Blending

Step 1

Step 2

Step 3

Stroke blending enables you to soften an array of colors together with a flat brush and a simple technique. Just use a vertical stroke to pull color from top to bottom, then reverse the process and move from the bottom to the top in one fluid motion.

Step 1: Holding your brush firmly between the tip of your thumb and index finger, angle it so the chisel edge and some of the hairs touch the wet painting surface. Now, starting at the top of your object, lightly pull the brush down, blending the colors together as you move the brush.

Step 2: Continue stroke blending, following the object's natural shape until the colors meld together. Remember to keep your strokes light—too much pressure will wipe all the paint from your surface. Clean your brush by wiping it on a paper towel after every few strokes.

Step 3: Additional color may be added as you continue stroke blending an object. Simply pick up color on your brush and lay it over the areas you've already blended, following the same stroke direction as before. After you've stroked from the top of the object to the bottom, reverse the process for a continuous shift in color.

Alizarin Crimson + Cadmium Yellow Light = Mud!

Alizarin Crimson + Cadmium Red Light

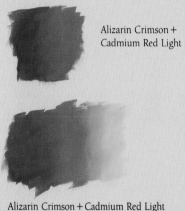

Alizarin Crimson + Cadmium Red Light + Cadmium Yellow Light

Be careful not to leap from your darkest to lightest color with no intermediary value, as in the top row. The middle row shows a perfect gradation of only two colors, while the bottom row shows successful blending of the top two colors with an intermediary value.

Blending Acrylics

Work quickly when blending acrylics, for it's the nature of acrylic paint to dry fast. There are, however, ways to slow the drying time.

- Keep your painting room cool. High humidity helps too.
- Don't paint near a fan, air vent or other source of circulating air.
- Use a moist rag for wiping your brush. If you wipe your brush on a dry rag when blending, you're simply drying the paint on your brush.
- Chill the water in your brush basin.
- Don't use a hair dryer to dry any part of your acrylics, especially if you're working on wood. The surface will hold the heat, causing areas you're trying to blend to dry more rapidly.

Textural Blending

Step 1

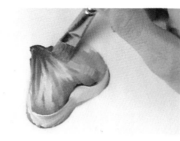

Step 2

Step 3

By blending layers of color with short, choppy strokes, you can add texture to any painted design. The textural blending technique is particularly effective for creating folds in drapery or ruffling flower petals as the brush strokes define the valleys and hills of the surface. Here's how to use this blending method:

Step 1: After you've base coated your object, add a second color using a flat brush and a patting motion.

Step 2: Holding the brush loosely, use light, choppy strokes to blend your color in the appropriate direction. Stroke the brush so that you're almost stopping as you blend.

Step 3: Finish blending by using the chisel edge of your brush to stroke out or pull down color following the contour of the object. This can create a rippled look, as shown in the flower petal at top right.

Blending Do's and Don'ts

Knowing when to quit blending comes with practice and with a little knowledge of some blending basics. To keep from ending up with choppy color transitions or over-blended "mud," follow these simple do's and don'ts:

- Don't apply too much paint to your surface. Start by loading your brush properly. Both the inner and outer bristles should be saturated but there shouldn't be excessive paint build-up on the outer edges of the brush or at the ferrule.
- Don't paint "too wet" or leave ridges of paint on the surface. Use only enough paint to adequately cover the surface.
- Do dry-wipe the brush after applying paint, before you blend the colors together.
- Do apply colors along a range of values from dark to light. When there's too great a disparity between the values of two blended colors, you'll create mud.
- Don't try to block in all the colors for an entire object and then come back to blend the values. This results in overblending. Instead, apply your dark value first and then the adjacent mid-value; blend, and then apply your light color and blend with the mid-value.
- Don't try to blend the lightest area with the darkest area. When blending, allow the brush to straddle and blend only over the break between the two colors.
- Do wipe over your painting lightly with a mop brush to remove obviously heavy brushstrokes.

Realistic Painting

One of the most useful skills for painters to master is the creation of form. Giving objects the appearance of depth and volume requires the control of value—the lightness or darkness of a color. Every object you paint should have a gradual change in value from light to dark to create its shape and form. Think of an apple: Painting a solid red circle would not describe the shape of the apple, nor give any hint of its depth and overall roundness. A real apple appears darker at the bottom and on the sides which move away from the light source, and lighter where the light source is closest—with one shade of red flowing evenly into another in a perfect gradation. If those value changes didn't exist, your apple would appear as if it all existed in one plane with no surfaces moving back into the distance and away from the light. So let's discover how value changes and blending techniques can help capture realism.

The shading and highlighting on these apples give them depth and form, making them appear realistic.

HOW VALUE CREATES FORM

In general, light values in a painting appear to come forward, and dark values appear to recede. An apple painted with shiny highlights, medium tones and dark shadows creates the illusion of form, depth and shape because the light areas appear closer while the dark areas move farther away.

The first step in creating form is to apply different values. This doesn't mean, however, that all you have to do is apply light, medium and dark values and your painted objects will have shape and form.

You also need to blend those values in a smooth gradation from light to dark. If you underblend your painting the object will still appear flat. In fact, until you create new values by blending between the originally applied values—and the lines where the colors meet are eliminated—no form and thus no realism will be established.

Take a look at the illustrations above. In square one, three colors are placed side by side. Each individual value appears flat, and the lightest

value (on the right) appears closest. In square two, the values have been carefully blended to create new values between the original three. (Don't blend so much that the values become blurred.) There's now a feeling of form and dimension that was absent before. The trick here is simple. To create form, an object must have light, medium and dark values, and these values must be blended along the lines where they meet.

Wet-on-Wet Painting

Use this technique for creating a blended, flowing look on a painting. This technique is generally used with water-based mediums, especially watercolors.

Step 1: Paint the base color, making sure it is fairly wet but opaque.

Step 2: While the base color is still wet, paint a color of the same or different value on top of it, blending or swirling the colors into each other or allowing them to bleed for a soft effect.

Step 1

Step 2

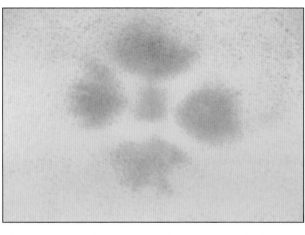

The wet-on-wet technique is great for creating cloudy skies, seascapes, and softly shaded fabric and flower petals, as well as interesting abstract designs.

Salt Resist

Salt can be used with watercolor paints and silk dyes. When added to wet paint, the granules break up the pigment and pull color toward them, creating a mottled effect.

Step 1: Lay down a wash of color. While the color is still wet, sprinkle the salt by hand or from a shaker onto the painting. Rock salt will create a more pronounced effect.

Step 2: Once the painting is dry, wipe away the salt with a piece of cardboard or stiff paper.

Step 1

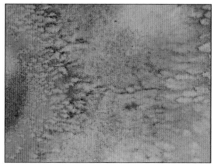

Step 2

Painting a Wash

A wash is paint that has been thinned to an ink-like consistency with water or a painting medium. The paint should be so thin that the pigment separates and the color becomes transparent. A wash is applied over a base coat to add color and give depth while still allowing the base tone to show through. To create a color wash, follow these steps:

Step 1

Step 2

Step 1: Begin by thinning your paint. For watercolors or acrylics, use water or a medium. For oils, use turpentine. Continue to add the medium until you form a watery, transparent layer of color.

Step 3

Step 2: To shade an object, such as a building or a landscape, apply a wash over an existing base color. The wash will easily glide over the surface because of its thin consistency and will deepen the base coat.

Step 3: You can also use a wash to add texture by applying it in choppy strokes.

Masking

Using frisket (masking fluid) is a simple way to protect white or light areas while you work on other areas of a painting. For instance, you can use masking fluid to protect pastel flower petals while painting a dark background around them. If you want to do a painting that requires small detail areas, intricate highlights or other shapes that need to remain white, frisket is the answer to your problems.

Step 1: Before placing your brush in masking fluid, dampen the hairs, then rub them against a bar of soap. This will help keep the hairs of your brush from being damaged by the frisket. Repeat this step frequently, always leaving soap on the brush while using the frisket. Gently stir the frisket (don't shake it, as air bubbles will form) and apply it to the area you wish to protect. Although frisket has a soft peach or blue color, it will not stain your painting. The coloration is simply there so you can easily see where you've applied the fluid. Immediately wash your brush in warm tap water after use.

Step 2: Allow the mask to dry completely before painting over or around it. It should feel rubbery when dry. Don't try to speed the drying time with a hair dryer, as the heat can bond the mask to the paper.

Step 3: Don't attempt to remove the frisket too soon—wait until the area around it is dry. The masking fluid should be removed very gently, using either a rubber cement eraser or a small piece of masking tape to slowly lift off the mask. Don't rip it off. Also, avoid pressing the tape

Step 1

Step 2

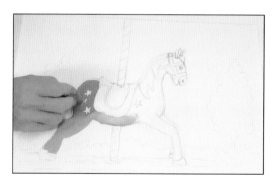

Step 3

down too hard, as it could damage the surrounding paper. Some papers are too soft to be used with frisket; when you remove the mask, they shred or tear. Since papers vary, it's a good idea to test the frisket on a scrap of the same paper you intend to use. (You shouldn't have any trouble with WestPort, Winsor & Newton, Lana, or Arches 140-, 260- or 300-lb. cold-pressed papers.)

Don't leave the mask on your paper for weeks at a time. If you need more time before you can paint again, remove the frisket and then reapply it later when you're ready to work. When the frisket is not in use, make sure you don't expose it to extreme temperatures—it will freeze or bake into a large jar of rubber.

Transferring a Pattern

There are several ways to transfer a design to wood and fabric. Experiment with a few to find your favorite method. It's always a good idea to trace or copy patterns before using to keep the original for later use.

TRANSFER PAPER

Step 1: Base coat your surface.

Step 2: Choose and prepare your transfer paper. If you use a light base coat color, you'll want to use gray transfer paper; a medium to dark base coat will require white transfer paper. Before using a new piece of transfer paper, you may wish to wipe the back with a paper towel dampened with turpentine. This will remove excess transfer material which may cause the pattern to transfer too strongly on the first few uses.

Step 3: Tape the transfer paper onto your surface, place the design on top of it and go over the pattern lines with a stylus or dried-out ballpoint pen, checking underneath one corner to be sure the correct side of the transfer paper is down and adjusting your pressure if lines are too light or dark. Remove smudges with a kneaded eraser.

CHALK TRANSFER

Step 1: Base coat your project and let dry.

Step 2: Turn over the traced design and draw over the pattern lines on the back with chalk. For light surfaces, use a medium-value, colored

chalk such as tan or gray; use white chalk on medium to dark surfaces. Shake off excess dust before taping the pattern to your surface.

Step 3: Go over the lines with a stylus or dried-out ballpoint pen. Remove messy lines or smudges from your surface with a kneaded eraser.

TRANSFER PENS AND PENCILS

Step 1: Trace the back of the pattern with the transfer pen or pencil.

Step 2: Tape the pattern to the surface right side up and press a warm iron on each area of the design for thirty seconds. Don't slide the iron over the design; instead, pick it up and replace it in a new area: Moving the iron may cause the pattern to shift out of place. The heat of the iron will cause the pen or pencil lines to adhere to the fabric.

DIRECT TRANSFER

This method is especially suited for thick, quilted fabrics.

Step 1: Make a tracing of your design, as this method will make cuts or holes in the pattern. Lay the tracing over the surface and tape it into position.

Step 2: Using a pencil with a sharp point, make short dash marks along the pattern lines, applying enough pressure to cut through the paper. When you have covered the whole design, remove the paper and connect the lines.

Transfer Paper
With a sheet of graphite paper under your pattern, go over the pattern lines with a stylus.

The design will transfer directly to the paper.

Chalk Method
Go over the lines on the back side of the pattern with chalk or graphite. Place the pattern right-side-up on your surface and trace the design with a stylus, as shown in the transfer paper illustration.

Another version of this method is to poke small holes along the pattern lines using a sharp pencil or upholstery pin. Attach the pattern to the surface, then rub over the lines with chalk or paint. When the pattern is removed, you can connect the dots with a pencil.

Cutting a Stencil

Although there are a wide variety of ready-cut stencil designs available today, cutting your own stencil gives you the opportunity to exactly match your pattern to a design found in your draperies, carpet or other furnishings in your room. Or maybe you're just feeling extra creative and want the satisfaction of knowing your stencil is a one-of-a-kind original. Either way, cutting your own stencil is surprisingly easy.

Step 1: Plan your design first, whether you are drawing it freehand or tracing the motif from a rug or curtain. If you are tracing from a pre-existing pattern, try to simplify the design to its basic elements. Be sure to leave space between the elements of the design, especially those which will be done in different colors. When you are happy with your pattern, retrace it onto a clean piece of paper, making sure all lines are smooth and exact.

Step 2: Tape the pattern securely under a sheet of transparent Mylar, waxed stencil paper or freezer paper. Then carefully cut along the lines using a sharp craft knife or an electrically heated stencil cutter. Use a metal ruler to ensure you stay true to straight lines. If you make a cut in the wrong place, you can repair it by placing clear tape over the front and back of the cut. Cut or file off jagged edges, as these will cause your stenciled design to look sloppy.

Step 3: Test your pattern on a brown paper bag or scrap paper to make sure all elements of the design transfer cleanly and are separated and sized as you desire. If you are unsure

Step 1

Step 2

Step 3

of your design or of the colors you've chosen, repeat the stencil several times on a long strip of kraft paper and tape it in place on your wall. Try

living with it for a day or two to make sure you really like it before it becomes a permanent feature of your decor.

Stenciling

Stenciling is a quick, attractive way to create a repeating pattern. It takes about a quarter of the time of hand-painting a design and looks equally terrific. This technique is ideal for decorating walls but can also be done on drapes, furniture and floors. You can use either a precut stencil or cut your own design as shown on page 63.

Step 1: Begin by adhering the stencil to your painting surface with low-tack masking tape. (Regular masking tape may peel paint off your walls; to remove some of the adhesive, stick each piece of tape to your shirt or pants several times before applying to your surface.) Load a round, stiff-bristled stencil brush with color and brush out the excess paint on a paper towel. Your brush should be very lightly loaded with color.

Step 2: Always begin your color application on the plastic surface of the stencil, gradually swirling the brush into the open areas. This avoids a dark blob of paint in your design each time you reload your brush. Apply pressure to the brush to scrub color onto the surface. You can also use sponge applicators to apply your stencil paints. With a barely saturated tip, color is "spounced" into the open area, giving a slightly textured effect. For an even easier application, try the newest foam rollers, which you simply roll in paint and then roll across the stencil pattern.

Step 3: If you are using more than one color in your stencil design, you may find it easiest to mask off all but the areas to be painted with your initial color and work those areas around the entire room or surface first. Then, when the first color is dry, you can go back and apply the areas with the second color and so on. Or you can complete each motif individually, filling in all the colors (and shading if desired), before moving the stencil to the next section. This eliminates the need to realign and reattach the pattern each time you switch colors.

To shade a stenciled area, load the stencil brush with a darker color and stroke over the outer edges of a section (photo 3A). Apply only a small amount of shading to an area. Before you remove the stencil completely, carefully lift a corner of it to check your color application (photo 3B). When you're satisfied with your work, pick up the stencil and position it next to the first one, following the guideline markings to place it correctly. Now, you're ready to repeat the stenciling process.

Step 1

Step 2

Step 3A

Step 3B

STENCILING TIPS

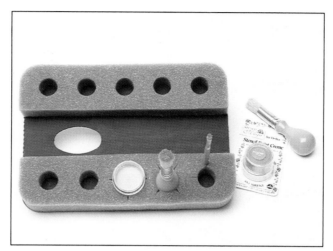

- Although stenciling is fairly easy to master, each stenciler must develop her own style. The best way to do so is to practice the pattern you intend to use on a long strip of paper before moving to a wall or other surface. Then you can tape the practice pattern onto the surface to make sure you like the design and pattern before you paint it. You'll avoid mistakes and save a lot of time this way.
- Use only one color per brush. The bristles on a stencil brush absorb too much paint to continually switch from one color to another.
- To repair a torn stencil, clean it and then place small pieces of transparent tape over the front and back of the stencil. Use a craft knife to carefully recut any open areas of the stencil covered by the tape.
- If you mix colors, mix enough for the entire project to ensure a consistent coverage of color.
- If an electrical outlet or telephone jack is in the path of a stenciled border, you can stencil right over it so you don't break the flow of the design, or use a decorative outlet cover which complements your design.
- Wearing an apron with several large pockets is a great way to keep supplies at hand and avoid trips up and down the ladder.
- If you get an area that's too dark, immediately dab it with a slightly damp rag or erase some of the paint with a kneaded eraser. If these methods don't work, simply paint over the area with the background color, let dry and stencil the design again.

- If you want to use only one part of the stencil, mask off the areas you don't want with low-tack tape. Be sure to remove the tape when finished.
- Clean the stencil surface whenever you stop to rest. This keeps paint from building up and making your colors muddy. Be careful not to let paint dry in your brushes when you quit working.
- Acrylic tube paints may need to be thinned before stenciling to make them more workable. If you thin your paints, be sure to test them on paper before moving to your surface to ensure that the paints aren't thinned to the point that they might bleed under the stencil.
- If you're doing an extensive wall stenciling project that will require you to be on a ladder for long periods of time, wrap upholstery foam around the rungs of the ladder so you have something soft to lean against. Also, try attaching adhesive-backed Velcro to the bottoms of your paint containers or palette and the top of the ladder; your paints will stay put right where you can reach them.

ℱAUX FINISHES

Although *faux* finishes can stand on their own as elegant works of art, they also make striking backgrounds for decorative paintings. In fact, throughout the history of decorative painting, *faux*-marble or *faux-bois* (false wood) effects have been combined with elaborate designs on all sorts of surfaces. Norwegian armoires often featured rosemaling with panels of *faux* marble. Dutch chests often included *faux* stone and marble effects. American colonial and Pennsylvania-Dutch folk art were often combined with *faux* woodgrains. And in America during the 1920s and 1930s, a line of furniture, often referred to as "cottage style," combined decorative painting in monochromatic tones with *faux* woodgrains and marbling. Full-color designs were often rendered right over a *faux* finish on cottage-style furniture, thus establishing the finish as a background element.

Today, we can combine new styles of decorative painting with the sophisticated look of *faux* finishes. Experiment with combinations of these two different painting styles to create unusual, unique looks.

TIPS FOR *FAUX* FINISHING

- Glaze walls with a partner; it makes the job easier.
- Glaze over a semi-gloss base coat instead of flat paint. Flat paint soaks up glaze like a sponge.
- Don't start glazing walls in the most noticeable area of a room. Start with inconspicuous spots to practice your technique.
- Use the cut end of a sea sponge for a soft look and the top end for a stippled look.
- Use subtle patterns and textures in small rooms; a bold pattern is too busy.
- Brush on the base coat, instead of rolling it on, for *strié* and *moiré* methods. A roller will leave marks.
- Use exotic finishes, such as tortoise and malachite, only in small doses; too much of a good thing looks unrealistic.
- Don't expect painted *strié* to be perfect. There will be variations and vertical lines.
- Don't treat an entire wall as one large piece of marble. Break up the wall into sections instead to look more realistic.

- Don't paint the veins in marble finishes like tree branches. Let them flow diagonally.
- Distress and antique pieces as little or as much as you want. Let your personal taste show.
- Use a different finishing technique on different sections of the same piece of furniture for more interest.
- Seal wood surfaces with a primer to prevent knots in the wood from showing through.
- Remove any tape used to mask out an area by pulling up and away from the paint to avoid peeling any paint off the surface.
- Experiment with new colors on a sample board before moving to the surface you intend to paint.
- Use painter's low-tack tape instead of regular masking tape; it won't pull up paint when you remove it.
- Don't comb entire walls. Combing looks best on smaller surfaces.
- Cut sponges to fit into tight areas, rather than sponging around them, which leaves an unpainted halo.
- Don't use unfamiliar products on heirloom pieces until you've tried them out on less valuable furniture or scrap surfaces first.

Verdigris

Verdigris finishes simulate the green patina that forms on such metals as copper, brass and bronze when exposed to air or saltwater. A realistic verdigris effect can be created with acrylic paints or by using one of many brush-on products or kits available today, such as Copper Topper and Patina Green (follow manufacturer's instructions for these products).

Step 1: Prime the surface to seal and protect, then stipple a base coat of black acrylic paint. Let dry, then apply another base coat. Thoroughly stir a bottle of copper metallic paint and pour some into a tub.

Step 2: Using a base coat bristle brush and random crisscross strokes, apply the copper paint to the surface. Let dry.

Step 3: Choose or mix a greenish-blue acrylic paint and pour into another tub. Now apply a second coat of copper paint to the surface, using a stippling motion. While this coat is still wet, use a natural sea sponge to apply the green patina color over the copper. Dab the sponge randomly onto the surface, turning it frequently to prevent a pattern from forming (see page 77 for more information on sponging). Allow some copper areas to show through.

Step 4: Allow the paint to dry thoroughly. Sponge more copper or green into any areas that have too much of one color. If a truly weathered look is desired, add a light stippling of thinned white paint to a few areas as a finishing touch.

Gold Leafing

Gold leafing is a method for adding shimmering metallic borders, backgrounds or designs to decorative works of art. Gold, silver and copper leaf are available in books of twenty-five 3″ × 3″ sheets, with tissue in between. Gold leaf can be applied over stained or painted wood, painted and sealed tin, glass, and fired or sealed ceramic. Just remember to begin the gold leafing process with a clean, smooth, lightly-sealed surface.

Step 1: Outline the area you want covered in gold leaf with chalk. If you're following a pattern, use tracing paper and chalk or transfer paper.

Step 2: As an optional step, you can paint a background color on the areas that will receive the leaf. This isn't necessary but looks nice if you leave cracks between the pieces of leaf either purposely or by mistake. Earth-tone colors, from golds to browns, are good for backgrounds.

Step 3: While the base color is drying, tear out the number of sheets you need from the book and lay them with the shiniest side up. With the tissue paper in between, tear the leaf into smaller pieces, but avoid over-handling them since they can be affected by the oils on your hands. I recommend working with small pieces, regardless of the size of your overall area of application, because they're easier to place and create interesting patterns.

Step 4: Stir a leaf adhesive sizing gently so air bubbles don't form, then use a brush to coat only the areas where you want leafing. If you

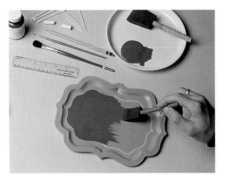

Chalk in the shape of the area to be gold-leafed. Apply a background color if desired.

Tear the sheet of gold leaf into smaller pieces.

Begin applying the gold leaf when the sizing becomes tacky.

Remove overlapping edges by brushing lightly with a mop brush. When complete, buff the surface with a soft cloth.

get the sizing where you don't want it, clean the area immediately with a bit of soap and water on a cotton swab or an old brush.

Step 5: When the sizing becomes tacky (after thirty to sixty minutes), begin applying the gold leaf. Carefully pick up each small piece of leaf with the tissue intact, handling it at the corners. (Tweezers are useful for small pieces.) On large designs, work from the center out. If you have a dark base tone, you can leave small spaces between the sheets. If you don't want spacing between the sheets, place each sheet slightly over the former. Don't worry about these overhanging pieces yet; just con-

tinue applying the leaf until the area has been covered. Allow this to dry for six to twelve hours.

Step 6: To remove the overlapping edges, lightly wipe the surface with a soft mop brush. This will pull off only the pieces that aren't glued on. Clean the brush occasionally. When done, lightly buff the surface.

Step 7: Before painting, antiquing or handling, seal the leafing with several light mists of clear acrylic sealer. Remember that several light applications are always better than one heavy coating. With the surface sealed, you can complete your piece with paint.

Marbleizing

With the marbleizing technique, you can make almost any surface look like marble—including tabletops, mantels, lamp bases and inset wall panels. The following steps show you how to create white alabaster marble; however, you can substitute colors to create pink, black or green marble also.

Step 1: Choose a medium-value gray oil paint to use as your base coat. Paint the marbling surface with the gray, then let dry. Load the tip of a feather with a mixture of Payne's Gray, Raw Umber and turpentine. Apply the marble's vein markings by stroking the feather in a "nervous," wiggling motion at a diagonal to the surface. Be sure to make the veins continuous around the edges of your surface.

Step 2: Load the feather with a little more of the gray color, then bend it back with your finger to fling on a few random specks of color.

Step 3: Create a glaze by thinning white oil paint with turpentine until it becomes transparent. After the vein markings have dried, apply this glaze of white over them, using a large brush. The glaze will begin to make the veins look like they're imbedded in the marble.

Step 4: Apply three more coats of the glaze mixture to the surface, allowing each coat to dry thoroughly before applying another. You'll see the veins fading into the surface.

Step 1

Step 2

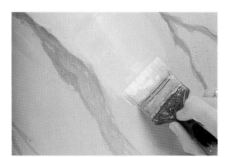

Step 3

Step 4

Wood Graining

Wood graining allows you to create the look of richly grained wood on any surface. Enhance an ordinary wall with "wood" panels, or give pressboard and other inexpensive pieces the look of expensive hardwoods such as mahogany or walnut.

To create the look of wood, first decide what type of wood pattern you want and choose the appropriate graining tool. Graining tools consist of rubber grooves (each one with different grooves to imitate a particular wood) attached to a mallet-like handle. These easy-to-use tools first became popular in the eighteenth century when artists used *faux* wood finishes on walls, floors, doors, furniture, wainscoting and chair rails.

Step 1

Step 2

Step 3

Step 4

Step 1: Apply a middle-value base coat (a tan hue) to your graining surface and let dry. Create a glaze using turpentine to thin the oil color you want to use for the wood grain. Earth tones such as Burnt Umber and Burnt Sienna work well for realistic wood-graining effects. Blend the paint until it has a thin, creamy consistency. Be careful not to add too much turpentine, however, because the mixture will dry too fast.

Step 2: Using a sponge or bristle brush, apply the glaze mixture over the base coat color with smooth, even strokes.

Step 3: Place the wood grain tool at the top of the wet surface and begin pulling and dragging it downward. As you stroke with the tool, rotate it so the grain pattern changes within a strip. When you begin the next section, hold the tool at a different angle than you did at the beginning of the first strip. Doing this will help you avoid repeating the same patterns beside each other.

Step 4: Soften the wood grain pattern by lightly dusting over it with a mop brush. Finally, wipe out a few highlights with a brush moistened with turpentine.

Combing

Combing is a technique that allows you to create an interesting pattern of lines on a surface—even walls and floors. Rubber, plastic and metal combs designed specifically for this technique are available at art supply stores. For smaller projects, you can also make homemade combs with poster board. The techniques can be done with water-based or oil-based paints.

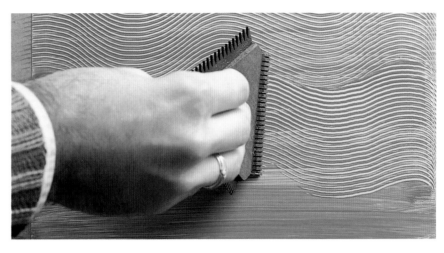

Step 1: Apply a base coat in the color of your choice and let dry. Next create a glaze by thinning your paint with the appropriate solvent (water or turpentine). Apply the glaze to the surface.

Step 2: While the glaze is still wet, drag the comb across the glaze, holding it at a slight angle. Comb in straight lines, create a wavy texture by dragging the comb in a curving motion, or create a basket-weave pattern by combing even-sized squares first horizontally, then vertically.

Strié

The *strié* technique is very similar to combing, except that a large brush is used to texture the glaze rather than a comb. The resulting pattern is a series of irregular, linear streaks. *Strié* works well on both walls and furniture.

Step 1: Base coat your surface with the color of your choice. When dry, mix clear painting glaze with the oil color of your choice, or use a commercially prepared glaze. Using a bristle brush, apply the glaze to the surface. For large projects and walls, glaze only as much as you can texture before the paint dries, then move to the next area.

Step 2: Using a flogger brush, stroke from top to bottom in one continuous motion to create the subtle appearance of lines, keeping the brush perpendicular to the surface.

Step 1

Step 2

Antiquing

If you like the rich look of old furniture and accessories but don't have a home filled with antiques, don't fret. You can make your decorative painted items look like heirlooms with an antiquing glaze. To glaze or antique a project, apply a thin coat of dark oil color to the surface, then rub part of it off. The result? You'll get the darkened look of age without waiting fifty years.

There are a number of antiquing methods available; each lends a different look and requires a different amount of time. They're all quite easy to accomplish no matter what your experience level, so choose the method best suited to your project.

INSTANT ANTIQUING METHOD

This quick and easy method was used to antique the potpourri heart boxes shown on this page. The beauty of the instant method is that you can add more glaze or remove a coat quickly to get the look you want. You can also use acrylic paint with this method. The surface will look streaked and a bit harsher, but it's a fine country finish, especially for small projects.

Instant Antiquing
With this method, you can antique your project a little or a lot. To tone down the bright colors on the finished box (top), a glaze was applied and then rubbed off, leaving dark areas around the edges only (middle). To create a darker antiqued look, the glaze coat was lightly and evenly wiped, leaving an overall-aged finish (bottom).

Step 1: When your decorative painting is thoroughly dry, apply two coats of a water- or oil-based varnish. Let this dry overnight before antiquing. Applying varnish over your painting gives you flexibility in controlling the degree of antiquing.

Step 2: You can use a commercial antiquing glaze or liquid, available in most craft stores, or mix your own. (Simply mix one part Burnt Umber or similar oil color to one part mineral spirits until the glaze reaches the consistency of heavy whipping cream.) Smoothly apply the glaze over your entire surface with an inexpensive 1″ brush. Allow to dry only until the shine is gone, about fifteen to twenty minutes.

Step 3: Using a soft cloth, wipe off the excess glaze in the direction of the wood grain.

Step 4: Brush over the surface in the same manner with a house paint bristle brush to soften the cloth wiping lines. At this point you can also rub off the glaze in places to create highlights. Let dry for twenty-four hours.

Step 5: Apply two to three coats of varnish, and let dry overnight.

THREE- TO SIX-DAY METHOD

Although it takes longer, the fine, polished finish you get with this method makes it the best choice for a piece you want to last a lifetime.

Step 1: When your decorative painting is thoroughly dry, brush on two coats of varnish. Let dry overnight.

Step 2: Brush on the antiquing glaze and allow to dry until the shine is gone, then pat the wood with a soft cloth to pick up any excess glaze.

Step 3: Brush the surface vigorously with a soft bristle brush until the entire surface has an even tone.

Step 4: After three or more days, use a steel wool pad and a little linseed oil to polish the surface, leaving the edges dark. Rub the wool in a circular motion, noting the subtle value variations that are created when you rub off different amounts of the glaze. Create highlights by removing all the glaze in one area. Work slowly and use a soft cloth to wipe off the residue that accumulates on the surface or the steel wool. If you remove too much glaze, pat on a little more until you achieve the look you want.

Step 5: When you're satisfied with the shading, put the project aside for twenty-four hours. Then wipe the surface with a cloth and apply two or three coats of varnish. Let dry at least forty-eight hours, then rub the surface with steel wool. Apply paste floor wax and buff with a soft rag to polish.

Three- to Six-Day Antiquing
Although it takes longer, the rich, heirloom quality of the finished cabinet (at right) is worth the extra time.

FINGER ROUGING METHOD

Rouging is great if you want rich antiquing along the edges or in small areas of a project. You don't need to mix any glaze—just use Burnt Umber, Raw Umber or Ivory Black oil color straight from the tube.

Step 1: Apply two coats of varnish and allow to dry, as with the other methods.

Step 2: Spread the oil color around the edges of your project with a soft cloth wrapped around your finger, using a circular motion. Rub the paint so that the value becomes lighter and softer toward the inside. If you don't like the results, remove the color immediately with mineral spirits and try again.

Finger Rouging
To add a quick antiqued touch around the edges of a project, or to further darken corners of a piece to which glaze has already been applied (as shown here), simply apply straight oil or acrylic paint to the edges with your finger.

Pickling

A pickling stain is a thinned white or light-colored paint mixture which allows the wood grain beneath it to show through. White Lightning wood sealer is commonly used to seal and pickle projects at the same time.

Step 1: Sand the wood, then wipe away any dust with a tack cloth.

Step 2: You can either create your own pickling stain, or use a commercial stain. To make your own, combine gesso, water-based varnish and water in equal proportions. Using a sponge or wide, flat brush, apply one coat of the stain to the wood to seal it, then let dry.

Step 3: Now, create another stain by combining the acrylic color of your choice with varnish and water. You can also create a tint for the White Lightning by mixing it with one to two drops of your favorite acrylic color.

Step 4: Use a slightly damp sponge brush to apply the stain to the wood using long, flowing strokes that move in the direction of the grain. Be sure to stroke from edge to edge to avoid stop marks. For a deeper tint, add more color; add more gesso or White Lightning for a lighter tint.

Step 5: Let dry, then finish with several coats of a water-based varnish.

Some color ideas for pickling stains: left, Robin's Egg Blue; center, Bright Celadon Green; right, Light Rose Pink.

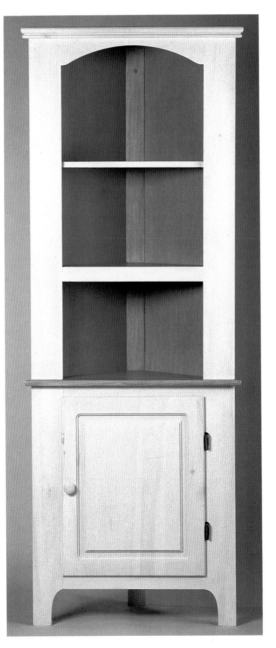

This cabinet was pickled with a cool white wash. Note how the subtle color application allows the wood grain to show through.

Crackling

This technique creates the appearance of old, weathered, cracking paint. The results can be distinctly different, depending on the product you use. Experiment with specially formulated products to find the one you like best. Here are two to try:

DecoArt's Weathered Wood produces a heavily aged, distressed finish.

SUBTLE CRACKLE FINISH

Step 1: Apply Jo Sonja's Crackle Medium or a similar product on a finished project. With a large soft brush, work to cover the surface in all directions, while keeping the coverage as thin as possible.

Step 2: Dry the surface with a hair dryer set on medium heat, moving it constantly over the surface until the finish is dry to the touch. You'll see fine cracks appear as the medium dries.

Step 3: To show off the crackled finish, apply an antiquing glaze over it, allowing it to cure overnight before finishing with several coats of varnish.

HEAVILY DISTRESSED FINISH

Step 1: Apply DecoArt's Weathered Wood medium over a dry base coat color with a large flat brush. The base coat will show through the cracks that form in the overcoat.

Step 2: Allow to set according to the directions (usually twenty to thirty minutes) and then immediately apply the overcoat, which causes the finish to crackle.

Step 3: Allow the project to cure overnight before applying two to three coats of varnish.

Create an elegant effect by applying a dark top coat over a metallic undercoat.

Tip

To create the look of old barn wood, try using a black base coat and a gray overcoat, antiquing if desired with Burnt Umber. You can also create an elegant look by painting a rich dark color over a metallic base coat. However, metallic paint can't be used as the overcoat because it won't crack.

Ragging and Rag Rolling

Step 1

Step 2

Step 3

Using a crumpled rag, you can create the illusion of a textured surface on a painting or wall. A rag finish is created by dipping a bundled rag in paint and pushing it against your surface in alternating patterns. You can also use a dry rag to lift paint off of a freshly painted surface, thereby creating a "negative" textured finish.

Rag rolling involves crumpling the rag into a cylindrical form. For positive rag rolling, dip the entire rag in paint and then roll the rag over the surface. Negative rag rolling is similar, but a dry rag is rolled over wet paint to lift the paint off of the surface.

The heavily textured, patterned effects you create with these techniques look great on walls, ceilings, trunks, floors and tabletops. Keep in mind that different types of fabric will create different patterns.

Step 1: Base coat your painting surface with the color of your choice and let dry. Choose a piece of fabric to blot or roll over the surface.

Step 2: Create a glaze by mixing oil paint with turpentine until it reaches the consistency of ink. Apply the

Ragging creates an intricate textured finish.

glaze on top of the base coat to create a negative effect.

Step 3: To create a rolled effect, roll the rag into a slender tube (like a rolling pin) and sprinkle it with turpentine. Pressing the flats of both your hands on the rag, roll it across the surface, creating a varying pattern. Once you've completed a couple of rows, unroll the rag and re-roll it so you have a fresh area to

This "negative" effect was created by lifting paint off with a dry, crumpled rag.

work with. Re-wet the rag and again roll it over the surface. For a ragged effect, crumple the rag into a loose ball and press in into the wet paint, varying the pattern and recrumpling the rag often.

To create additional texture on your rolling, you can sprinkle drops of turpentine directly on the surface. The turpentine will dissolve and mix with the wet glaze color.

Sponging

Sponging is a simple but effective way to add a textured look to your walls, furniture and fabric. You can sponge on one color over a base coat, apply several different colors over a base, or sponge on a dark, medium and light value of one color.

Step 1

Step 1: Before you begin sponging, apply a base coat color to your surface. Use a brush for small surfaces and a paint roller for larger areas.

Step 2: Thin your paint to the consistency of a wash (use water to thin acrylics and turpentine for oils). Dip a natural sea sponge in the mixture, then blot it on a paper towel. Using medium pressure, randomly dab the sponge on the surface. Be sure to constantly turn the sponge after you lift it so you don't repeat the sponge's

hole pattern. Let dry.

Step 3: If you like, you can now apply a second layer of sponging. Use the same color wash to intensify your first sponging, or apply a new color as shown in the photo. Experiment with your sponge on a piece of paper before you use it on your painting surface.

Step 3

Plastic Wrap Texturing

Step 1

Step 2

Finished texture.

The plastic wrap texturing technique creates a heavily patterned effect that you can use on a variety of items.

Step 1: Apply a base color, keeping in mind that this shade will be seen through the textured pattern. Create a glaze of turpentine, varnish and

linseed oil in a 4:2:1 ratio. Mix thoroughly, then add oil paint to color it. Brush on (a section at a time in larger areas) using a sponge brush or soft bristle brush.

Step 2: Crumple a large piece of plastic wrap into a ball and release it

slightly. Begin "hitting" the surface with the plastic wrap, moving and turning the plastic over to fresh areas. After the wrap is coated with color, start over with a new ball of plastic.

Spattering ("Flyspecking")

Spattering is a great decorating technique to use for a loose, lightly sprayed look. It's ideal for decorating furniture, baseboard and trim areas, wainscoting and more. In a painting, it can also be used to create falling snow effects.

Step 1: Thin your paint (any color) to the consistency of ink, using water for acrylics or turpentine for oils. Fully load an old toothbrush with the mixture.

Step 2: Holding the brush over the surface, run your thumb or palette knife toward you over the bristles of the toothbrush, allowing random specks of paint to fall onto the surface. The closer you are to the surface, the larger and heavier the spattering will be. Move farther away from your surface to create a lighter mist of specks. For a soft, muted effect, spatter paint onto a wet surface. The paint will dissolve and spread out when it hits the surface.

Hold the brush closer for heavier spatters.

Hold the brush farther away for a lighter mist of specks.

Spatter onto a wet surface for a soft effect.

Use flyspecking to add interest or a slightly aged look to gilded or painted surfaces.

Stippling

Stippling is a fun brush technique you can use to add "fuzzy" texture to any surface. It's easy to do because it involves randomly dabbing paint onto your surface. It's perfect for backgrounds, sections of furniture, plates and accessories, and can add texture and coarseness to your paintings.

Step 1: Apply a base coat color to the surface—either light, medium or dark value. The base coat can be either a smoothly applied surface or a stippled base area.

Step 2: Load the largest coarse-haired brush you can fit comfortably on your surface with a color that contrasts to the base coat. Use an old brush with hairs that no longer join together to form a chisel edge. Begin dabbing or "pouncing" the brush on the surface while constantly moving it around the area to be covered. Pick up additional colors at any time to add interest and texture. To create depth, add a middle value color over the darker base stippling and a highlight or light value in a small area or center of interest.

Step 1

Step 2

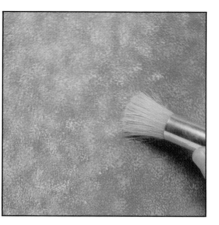

Stipple on additional colors to create more texture.

Create depth when stippling in a painting by adding different values.

𝒯RICKS OF THE TRADE

Here are thirty-four useful tips on everything from cleaning up spills to studio safety from some of the top decorative artists in the country.

CLEANING BRUSHES

1. Ginger Edwards: After cleaning your oil-painting brushes in turpentine or brush cleaner, work a little baby or vegetable oil into them. Wipe the brush on a soft cloth or towel—the oil will remove any residual paint still in the hairs. In addition, rub the oil on your hands to clean and soften them after painting.

2. Priscilla Hauser: To clean acrylic brushes, I like to use Shaklee's Basic H. I've found it's good for cleaning all kinds of things. After you've finished cleaning the brush, just leave the Shaklee's in the hairs, shape the bristles and store so that none of the hairs are bent or pushed out of shape. Rinse the brush with water before you use it again.

3. Dorothy Egan: Don't clean your brushes in the palm of your hand— you'll be rubbing harmful pigments into your skin. To clean my brushes, I stroke them on a bar of Ivory soap—that way, I can easily tell when they're clean. I then put lard

oil in them to recondition them.

4. Susan Scheewe: If your brushes are out of shape, clean them in hot water, then rub them over the glue section of an envelope, leaving the glue on the brushes to reshape them. Before painting, rinse out the water-soluble glue.

5. Andy B. Jones: You can remove dried paint from acrylic brushes with fingernail polish remover or acetone. Work the acetone into the brush until the paint dissolves, then wash the brushes with soap and water.

6. Brenda McPeek: When stenciling with multiple colors, rub the brushes you're not using on a baby wipe, then wrap them in wet wipes to keep them from drying out. To clean a brush for a new color, wipe it thoroughly on a baby wipe, then dry it on a paper towel.

REJUVENATING A TACK CLOTH

7. Jackie Shaw: To rejuvenate a tack cloth, place it in a plastic bag and sprinkle it with a small amount of spirit-based varnish thinned with turpentine. Close the bag and knead the cloth to work the varnish and turpentine into the fibers. Store the cloth in an airtight jar for several days to let the mixture permeate the cloth.

REMOVING PAINT

8. Deanne Fortnam: To get acrylic paint out of your clothes, try Simple Green, made by Sunshine Makers, Inc. Spray it on full strength, then let it sit for about fifteen minutes. Use a toothbrush to scrub out the paint. Simple Green is also great for cleaning out dirty brush basins, and it's nontoxic and biodegradable.

9. Priscilla Hauser: To remove dried oil paints from your clothing, spray a little Mr. Muscle Oven Cleaner on the spot. (First be sure to test the spray for colorfastness on an inconspicuous area of the clothing.) Let the cleaner set for five to ten minutes, then use an old, soft toothbrush to gently brush the paint out of the fabric.

10. Ann Kingslan: I've found that a kneaded eraser is a wonderful tool for removing mistakes from your oil paintings. Just work the eraser in your hands into the approximate shape of the mistake. Then, press the eraser down into the wet paint to remove the error.

11. Jackie Shaw: You can safely remove dried acrylic paint from countertops and tables by scraping it with an old credit card.

12. Dorothy Egan: Rub a barrier cream like Winsor & Newton's Artguard into your hands when painting or antiquing. The cream makes clean-up easy—all you have to do is wash your hands.

VANISHING PATTERN LINES

13. Gayle Laible: When painting with acrylics or other water-based paints, use mineral spirits to easily remove graphite tracing lines. Disappearing fabric markers can also be used to draw designs on wood, paper and other surfaces, leaving no tracing lines once you paint over the ink.

EXTENDING DRYING TIME

14. Priscilla Hauser: When painting with acrylics, always work with both a wet rag and a dry rag on which to wipe your brush. If you wipe your brush on a wet rag, it won't dry out quite as fast and will actually keep the acrylic paint wet a little longer.

15. Susan Scheewe: To slow the drying time of acrylic tube paint, apply a few drops of glycerin to each color or to your water container.

16. Jackie Shaw: To keep acrylic paints fresh on your palette, place a wet, folded paper towel along the edge of the palette and squeeze paints onto the damp towel. For additional longevity, mist the paint with a spray bottle, or dip an old toothbrush or stencil brush into water and spatter moisture over the paint.

BLENDING OILS

17. Phillip C. Myer: If you're having a hard time getting your oil colors to blend smoothly, try adding some Japan drier to the paint. When the paint becomes slightly tacky, the colors can then easily be brushed to create the slick, blended look you want.

FINISHES

18. Sherry Nelson: If you base coat a project with acrylic paint, you can varnish it with either oil- or water-based varnish. But if you base coat with oil paint, you must only use oil-based varnish over it. Even though some paint companies say you can use water-based varnish over oil paint, I've found that it never lasts.

19. Jackie Shaw: I've found that white or clear shellac is a great wood sealer. Available at hardware stores, shellac is inexpensive and seals wood so well that sap doesn't leak through. Plus, shellac dries in only thirty minutes. An extra bonus when using shellac is that you don't have to clean your brush out after you use it—just let it dry. The hairs will harden, but once you touch the brush to shellac again, they'll soften. But be sure to check the expiration date—shellac does have a limited shelf life. Don't buy a gallon if you only need a little.

20. Deanne Fortnam: After painting and varnishing a mailbox that will be kept outdoors, apply a coat of ordinary car wax to it every now and then. The wax will clean and shine the metal and protect your painted design from the elements.

21. Donna Bryant Waterson: For a smooth wax finish on your wood creations, try Kiwi Natural Shoe Polish. Saturate a piece of steel wool with the polish, rub it over your project and buff.

22. Brenda McPeek: Spraying projects with a matte finishing spray can leave a grit on your surface. Rather than painting directly over this grit, first wipe the surface of your project with a crumpled tack cloth.

STORING WATERCOLOR PAPERS AND PAINTS

23. Betty Denton: Store watercolor paper flat, away from excessive heat or moisture. Use a loose cover on moist watercolor palettes; sealing them air-tight could cause mold to grow in the paint.

HANDY LIDS

24. Brenda McPeek: Save the "squirt" tops from syrup and dish detergent bottles to replace messy lids on jars of blending and glazing mediums.

CHOOSING COLORS

25. Ann Kingslan: Selecting colors for a painting project is quite similar to getting dressed. Just as you would choose formal dress for a symphony and casual attire for a picnic, you should choose colors that match the mood or theme of your project. A painting will look formal when done in dark, heavy colors with glistening or metallic accents, while light or pastel tones will suggest a casual feel. Certain colors will be automatically associated with a particular style; for example, slate blue and off-white suggest a country feel while deep browns and dusky roses are reminiscent of the Victorian era.

26. DeLane Lange: If you have a difficult time choosing colors for your projects, gather a collection of wallpaper sample books, greeting cards, wrapping paper and other resources to inspire you. Write down the colors in designs you find appealing, thinking about the ratio in which colors appear. Use these colors and ratios for your projects.

MARIBETH STONE'S SAFETY TIPS

27. Don't eat or drink in your painting area, or use paints near food. Toxic dusts and particles are easily ingested by hand or mouth contact. For this reason, don't paint on your kitchen table or put a paintbrush—even the handle end—into your mouth.

28. Make sure your work area is well-ventilated. Always open a window or use a circulating fan when painting. This is especially important when using oil paints with thinners and harsh solvents.

29. Aerosols should only be used outdoors, and then only when wearing a disposable dust mask. Dangerous chemicals in spray paint, varnish, fixatives and adhesives remain in the air long after they've been sprayed.

30. Never pour solvents or acrylic paints down the drain. Ideally, you should save them in a jar and take them to your nearest hazardous waste disposal site. If you can't get to such a site, soak up the liquids with paper towels and discard these in your garbage.

31. Read all labels carefully. Avoid products containing benzene (benzol) and carbon tetrachloride, as they are extremely toxic. Follow the storage instructions carefully, as many products are highly flammable or sensitive to temperature changes. Watch for warnings such as "skin irritant" and "use with proper ventilation." Nontoxic does not mean a product can be ingested or inhaled Use safety precautions for these products as you would with any other art material.

32. Keep all art supplies out of the reach of children.

33. Use mineral spirits or odorless thinner instead of turpentine. Wear protective gloves when using any solvent. If your skin comes in contact with a solvent, wash the area immediately with soap and water.

34. Don't smoke around paints and solvents. Many of these products are highly flammable.

Oil to Acrylic Color Conversion Guide

Converting a project from oil paints to acrylic colors can be a frustrating task, especially if you don't know what the oil color listed looks like. The charts on pages 86 and 87 convert some of the most commonly used oil colors into six popular brands of acrylic paint. To achieve the transparent effect created by some oil colors (shown at the bottom edge of the color swatches), thin your acrylic paints with water and apply the paint as a wash. Achieving the correct ratio of colors will come with practice and experimentation. Add the most of the first color listed, gradually adding smaller amounts of the colors following until you achieve a color comparable to the swatch.

Chart Abbreviations *(for pages 86–89)*

Bl = Blue	Ox = Oxide
Br = Brown	Parch = Parchment
Cad = Cadmium	PHG = Permanent Hooker's
Cal = Calico	Green
Choc = Chocolate	PNC = Peaches n' Cream
Cob = Cobbler	Pk = Pink
Cof = Coffee	Pr = Prussian
Crim = Crimson	Rd = Red
CRL = Cadmium Red Light	RU = Raw Umber
CRM = Cadmium Red Medium	SB = Sapphire Blue
CYL = Cadmium Yellow Light	Scar = Scarlet
Dev = Devonshire	Sch = School
Diox = Dioxazine	South = Southern
Evergn = Evergreen	SW = Soft White
Fgrbry = Fingerberry	TB = Teddy Bear
Gr = Green	Tum = Tumbleweed
Hkbry = Huckleberry	Ultra = Ultramarine
Licr = Licorice	UT = Unbleached Titanium
Lt = Light	Vict = Victorian
Nap = Napthol	WW = Warm White
NG = Nimbus Gray	YO = Yellow Oxide
NO = Norwegian Orange	Yw = Yellow
Or = Orange	

 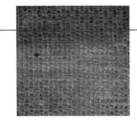  

OIL COLOR	*Alizarin Crimson*	*Asphaltum*	*Brownish Madder*	*Burnt Sienna*
AMERICANA	Nap Rd + True Blue	Cad Or + Kelly Gr + Raw Sienna	Crim Tide + Brandy Wine	Burnt Sienna
ACCENT	Jo Sonja Rd + Pure Blue	Rd Apple + True Gr + Pure Yw	Barn Rd + Pure Rd + Fgbry Rd	Burnt Sienna + Barn Rd
CERAMCOAT	Mendocino	Autumn Brown	Burgundy Rose	Burnt Sienna
FOLKART	Cherry Royale	Cal Rd + Evergrn + Sch Bus Yw	Barnyard Red	Hkbry + Nutmeg + Cof Bean
JO SONJA	Burgundy + Nap Crim	Raw Sienna + Burnt Umber	Rd Earth + Cad Scar + Nap Crim	Burnt Sienna
LIQUITEX	Alizarin Crimson	Raw Sienna + Burnt Umber	Burgundy + Burnt Umber	Burnt Sienna

OIL COLOR	*Cadmium Red Medium*	*Cadmium Yellow Deep*	*Cadmium Yellow Light*	*Cadmium Yellow Medium*
AMERICANA	Cad Rd + Crim Tide	Tangerine	Lemon Yw + Cad Yw	Cad Yellow
ACCENT	Pure Red	True Or + Pure Yw	Pure Yellow	Pure Yw + True Or
CERAMCOAT	Tompte	Yellow	Luscious Lemon	Bright Yellow
FOLKART	Christmas Rd	Glazed Carrots + Sch Bus Yw	Lemon Custard	Sch Bus Yellow
JO SONJA	Nap Rd Lt + Nap Crim + Rd Earth	Cad Yw Mid + Vermilion	Cad Yw Lt	Cad Yw Mid
LIQUITEX	Lacquer Rd + Rd Ox + Scar Rd	Brilliant Or + Brilliant Yw	Brilliant Yw + Yw Lt, Hansa	Brilliant Yellow

OIL COLOR	*Hansa Yellow Medium*	*Ivory Black*	*Lamp Black*	*Mauve*
AMERICANA	Cadmium Yellow	Ebony Black	Ebony Black	Burgundy Wine + True Blue
ACCENT	Sunkiss Yellow	Soft/Real Black	Soft/Real Black	Wineberry
CERAMCOAT	Bright Yw + Yw	Black + Charcoal	Black	Candy Bar
FOLKART	Sunny Yellow	Licorice	Licorice	Plum Pudding + Plum Chiffon
JO SONJA	Cad Yw Mid + Turner's Yw	Carbon Black	Carbon Black	Diox Purple + Indian Rd Ox
LIQUITEX	Brilliant Yellow	Ivory Black	Mars Black	Prism Violet + Burnt Umber

OIL COLOR	*Raw Umber*	*Sap Green*	*Titanium White*	*Ultra Blue*
AMERICANA	Dark Choc + Raw Sienna	Evergreen	Snow White	Ultra Blue Deep + Diox Purple
ACCENT	Raw Umber + Tumbleweed	Pine Needle Gr + True Gr	Soft/Real White	Pure Blue + True Blue
CERAMCOAT	Walnut	Christmas Gr + Phthalo Gr	White	Ultra Blue
FOLKART	Choc Fudge + Licorice	Green Meadow	Wicker White	Ultra
JO SONJA	Raw Umber	Pine Green	Titanium White	Ultra Blue Deep
LIQUITEX	Raw Umber	Hooker's Green	Titanium White	Ultra Blue

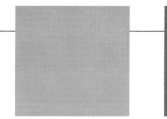
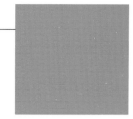

OIL COLOR	*Burnt Umber*	*Cadmium Orange*	*Cadmium Red Deep*	*Cadmium Red Light*
AMERICANA	Dark Choc + Ebony Black	Tangerine + Cad Or	Crim Tide	Cad Or
ACCENT	Real Umber	True Or + Pure Yw	Holiday Rd + Barn Rd	Pure Rd + True Or
CERAMCOAT	Burnt Umber	Orange	Maroon	Blaze
FOLKART	Choc Fudge + Cof Bean + Licr	Glazed Carrots + Sch Bus Yw	Cal Rd + Hkbry	Pimento + Sch Bus Yw
JO SONJA	Burnt Umber	Vermilion + Cad Yw	Nap Crim + Rd Earth	Cad Scarlet
LIQUITEX	Burnt Umber	Brilliant Orange	Nap Crim + Rd Ox	Scarlet Red

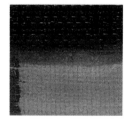

OIL COLOR	*Cerulean Blue*	*Chromium Oxide Green*	*Cobalt Blue*	*Davy's Gray*
AMERICANA	True Blue	Forest Green	Ultra Blue + Diox Purple	Charcoal + Charcoal Gray
ACCENT	Pure Blue + Ultra Blue	Gr Olive + Deep Forest Gr	Pure Blue	Soft/Real Black + Pine Needle
CERAMCOAT	Ocean Reef	Woodland Night	Ultra Blue	Hippo Gray Ceramcoat
FOLKART	Blue Ribbon	Old Ivy + Shamrock	Ultra	Licr + Poppy Seed
JO SONJA	Sapphire	Gr Ox + Teal Gr + Carbon Black	Cobalt Blue	Carbon Black + Pine Gr
LIQUITEX	Cerulean Blue	Chromium Ox Green	Brilliant Blue Purple	Ivory Black + Chromium Ox Gr

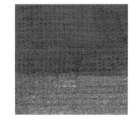

OIL COLOR	*Naples Yellow*	*Payne's Gray*	*Prussian Blue*	*Raw Sienna*
AMERICANA	Cad Yw + Burnt Or	Ebony Black + Ultra Blue Deep	Midnight Blue	Raw Sienna + Russet
ACCENT	Dijon Gold	Soft/Real Black + Pure Blue	Winsor Blue	Burnt Sienna + Tumbleweed
CERAMCOAT	Straw	Charcoal	Prussian Blue	Raw Sienna
FOLKART	Sch Bus Yw + Harvest Gold	Licr + Thunder Blue	Ultra Blue + Indigo	Maple Syrup + English Mustard
JO SONJA	Cad Yw Mid + Yw Ox + Vermilion	Payne's Gray + Carbon Black	Prussian Blue Hue	Raw Sienna + Rd Earth
LIQUITEX	Brilliant Yw + Yw Ox	Payne's Gray	Navy + Payne's Gray	Raw Sienna + Burnt Sienna

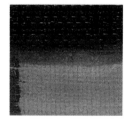

OIL COLOR	*Vermilion*	*Violet*	*Viridian*	*Yellow Ochre*
AMERICANA	Cad Or + Tangerine	Diox Purple + Nap Rd	Viridian	Antique Gold
ACCENT	True Or	True Purple + Jo Sonja Rd	Avon on the Gr	Golden Harvest + Tumbleweed
CERAMCOAT	Hallingdal Rd	Purple	Deep River + Phthalo Gr	Pig Skin
FOLKART	Autumn Leaves	Burgundy + Ultra	Wintergreen	Harvest Gold + Honeycomb
JO SONJA	Vermilion	Diox Purple + Nap Rd Lt	Teal + Phthalo Gr	Yellow Ox
LIQUITEX	Scar Rd + Brilliant Yw	Prism Violet	Phthalo Gr	Yellow Ox

Acrylic Color Matching Guide

No matter which brand of acrylic paints you use, there will always be occasions when a project calls for a brand or color name that you don't have. Rather than buying new paints for every project, use the chart below to find an equivalent color in a brand you already own. Matches are given for thirty-two popular acrylic colors with conversions for six well-known brands: Americana by DecoArt, Accent by Koh-I-Noor, Ceramcoat by Delta Technical Coatings, FolkArt by Plaid, Jo Sonja by Chroma Acrylics, and Liquitex by Binney & Smith.

If an exact match is not available from brand to brand, a mixture is suggested, followed by a mixture ra-tio (3:1 is three parts of the first color mixed with one part of the second color). A "T" in the ratio indicates only a touch is needed. If two colors are similar but one color is a shade darker, it's indicated with a (D); a color that's a shade lighter is indicated with an (L).

AMERICANA	Lemon Yellow	Cadmium Yellow	Taffy Cream	Antique Gold
ACCENT	Yellow Light	Sunkiss Yellow	Light Cactus Flower	Golden Harvest
CERAMCOAT	Luscious Lemon	Bright Yellow	Custard	Antique Gold
FOLKART	Lemon Custard	Sunny Yellow	Lemonade	Harvest Gold
JO SONJA	Cadmium Yellow Light	Cadmium Yellow Medium	Yellow Light + White 1:1	Yellow Oxide (D)
LIQUITEX	Yellow Light Hansa	Brillian Yellow/CYL Hue	White + Hansa Yellow 4:1	Yellow Oxide (D)

AMERICANA	Yellow Ochre	Pumpkin	Dusty Rose	Peaches 'n Cream
ACCENT	Dev Cream + Tum 6:1	True Orange + Razzle Red (T)	Victorian Mauve	Lt PNC + Pink Blossom 1:1
CERAMCOAT	Old Parch + Spice Tan 5:1	Pumpkin	Normandy Rose	Pink·Angel + White 6:1
FOLKART	Moon Yellow + TB Tan 6:1	Pure Orange	Sachet Rose	Peach Cob + Coral Reef 8:1
JO SONJA	WW + YO + Fawn 10:1:T	Vermillion + Yellow Light 3:1	WW + Red Earth + RU 3:1:T	White + NO + CYL 5:1:1
LIQUITEX	SW + YO + UT 10:1:1	Cadmium Orange	Deep Portrait Pk + White 1:1	Apricot + Lt Portrait Pink 1:1

AMERICANA	Brilliant Red	Brandy Wine	Cadmium Red	Burgundy Wine
ACCENT	Vermillion + Nap Red Lt 1:1	Barn Red + Fingerberry 2:1	Napthol Red Light	Pure Red + Bordeaux 1:1
CERAMCOAT	Nap Crimson + Orange 1:1	Burgundy Rose	Bright Red	Black Cherry
FOLKART	Red Lt + Nap Crimson 1:1	Huckleberry	Christmas Red + Red Lt 3:1	Cherry Royale
JO SONJA	Cadmium Scarlet	NO + Indian Red Ox 4:1	Napthol Red Light	Burgundy + Nap Red Lt 2:1
LIQUITEX	CRL + CRM 4:1	Red Ox + Burnt Sienna 1:1	CRM Hue/Lacquer Red	Burgundy + Lacquer Red 2:1

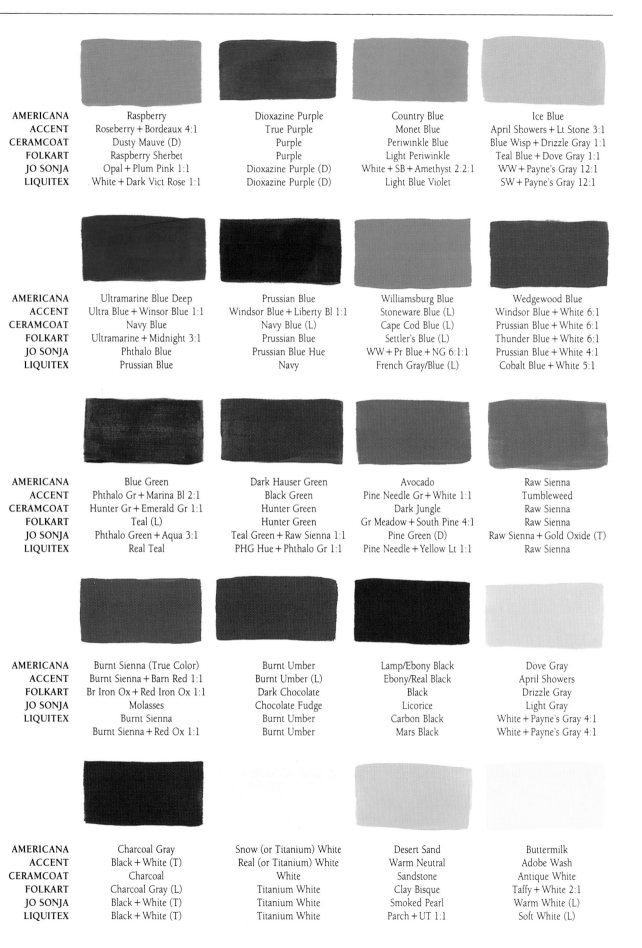

AMERICANA	Raspberry	Dioxazine Purple	Country Blue	Ice Blue
ACCENT	Roseberry + Bordeaux 4:1	True Purple	Monet Blue	April Showers + Lt Stone 3:1
CERAMCOAT	Dusty Mauve (D)	Purple	Periwinkle Blue	Blue Wisp + Drizzle Gray 1:1
FOLKART	Raspberry Sherbet	Purple	Light Periwinkle	Teal Blue + Dove Gray 1:1
JO SONJA	Opal + Plum Pink 1:1	Dioxazine Purple (D)	White + SB + Amethyst 2:2:1	WW + Payne's Gray 12:1
LIQUITEX	White + Dark Vict Rose 1:1	Dioxazine Purple (D)	Light Blue Violet	SW + Payne's Gray 12:1

AMERICANA	Ultramarine Blue Deep	Prussian Blue	Williamsburg Blue	Wedgewood Blue
ACCENT	Ultra Blue + Winsor Blue 1:1	Windsor Blue + Liberty Bl 1:1	Stoneware Blue (L)	Windsor Blue + White 6:1
CERAMCOAT	Navy Blue	Navy Blue (L)	Cape Cod Blue (L)	Prussian Blue + White 6:1
FOLKART	Ultramarine + Midnight 3:1	Prussian Blue	Settler's Blue (L)	Thunder Blue + White 6:1
JO SONJA	Phthalo Blue	Prussian Blue Hue	WW + Pr Blue + NG 6:1:1	Prussian Blue + White 4:1
LIQUITEX	Prussian Blue	Navy	French Gray/Blue (L)	Cobalt Blue + White 5:1

AMERICANA	Blue Green	Dark Hauser Green	Avocado	Raw Sienna
ACCENT	Phthalo Gr + Marina Bl 2:1	Black Green	Pine Needle Gr + White 1:1	Tumbleweed
CERAMCOAT	Hunter Gr + Emerald Gr 1:1	Hunter Green	Dark Jungle	Raw Sienna
FOLKART	Teal (L)	Hunter Green	Gr Meadow + South Pine 4:1	Raw Sienna
JO SONJA	Phthalo Green + Aqua 3:1	Teal Green + Raw Sienna 1:1	Pine Green (D)	Raw Sienna + Gold Oxide (T)
LIQUITEX	Real Teal	PHG Hue + Phthalo Gr 1:1	Pine Needle + Yellow Lt 1:1	Raw Sienna

AMERICANA	Burnt Sienna (True Color)	Burnt Umber	Lamp/Ebony Black	Dove Gray
ACCENT	Burnt Sienna + Barn Red 1:1	Burnt Umber (L)	Ebony/Real Black	April Showers
FOLKART	Br Iron Ox + Red Iron Ox 1:1	Dark Chocolate	Black	Drizzle Gray
JO SONJA	Molasses	Chocolate Fudge	Licorice	Light Gray
LIQUITEX	Burnt Sienna	Burnt Umber	Carbon Black	White + Payne's Gray 4:1
	Burnt Sienna + Red Ox 1:1	Burnt Umber	Mars Black	White + Payne's Gray 4:1

AMERICANA	Charcoal Gray	Snow (or Titanium) White	Desert Sand	Buttermilk
ACCENT	Black + White (T)	Real (or Titanium) White	Warm Neutral	Adobe Wash
CERAMCOAT	Charcoal	White	Sandstone	Antique White
FOLKART	Charcoal Gray (L)	Titanium White	Clay Bisque	Taffy + White 2:1
JO SONJA	Black + White (T)	Titanium White	Smoked Pearl	Warm White (L)
LIQUITEX	Black + White (T)	Titanium White	Parch + UT 1:1	Soft White (L)

GLOSSARY OF PAINTING TERMS

Acrylic color Powder pigment carried in a binder of acrylic polymer emulsion and water. These paints can be cleaned up or thinned with water, are extremely fast-drying, and form a durable, rubbery film when dry. Available in tubes, jars and squeeze bottles. Acrylics are sold in artist's, student and decorative/craft varieties.

Alkyd color A mixture of powdered pigments ground in synthetic resin, derived from glycerol and phthalic anhydride. Alkyds must be thinned and cleaned up with mineral spirits or turpentine. They dry much faster than oils, but slower than acrylics.

Antiquing The application of a thin glaze of dark color—usually brown or black oil paint—to create the appearance of age.

Artist's acrylic color A professional grade of acrylic paint made from pure powder pigment ground in acrylic polymer emulsions. Colors are true in the sense that a mixture of yellow and red will achieve a pure orange hue.

Artist's oil color A professional grade of oil color is made of powder pigment ground in linseed and other oils. Colors are true in the sense that a mixture of yellow and red will achieve a pure orange hue.

Base coat A smooth, even undercoat, applied to an entire surface prior to decorative painting, which serves as the base color of the design. Small areas within a design are also base coated with a toning color prior to dry brushing, painting washes, floating colors, etc.

Binder The agent in paints that adheres the powder pigments together.

Blending Mixing two or more colors on the wet surface of a painting to achieve a gradual color transition, using a brush and one of the various blending techniques.

Cold-pressed An artist's paper with a rough texture, good for drawing methods which require tooth to "grab" the medium, such as softer graphite, charcoal and pastels. Sometimes referred to as vellum and "not" pressed.

Color-book painting Filling in a design with solid, uniform areas of color, similar to the way a picture in a coloring book is completed. Shading, highlights and detail work can be added over color-booked designs.

Combing A finishing technique that uses a large plastic or metal comb to drag a linear pattern into a wet paint glaze.

Crackling Creating an aged, cracked or chipped paint effect by applying a crackling medium or hide glue over a base coat of paint. When a top coat of paint is applied, the medium prevents it from adhering to the surface, causing it to crack and separate, revealing the undercoat color.

Decorative and craft acrylic colors This grade of acrylic paints is often thinner and creamier than artist's acrylics and contains less pigment. Unlike artist's acrylics, craft acrylics aren't true hues but have been grayed to produce subtle color

variations. A mixture of yellow and red, for example, won't necessarily create a true, clean orange hue. The paints are usually packaged in jars and squeeze bottles.

Distressing Roughing up a wooden piece to give it an aged, weathered appearance using a hammer, ice pick, nail or other tool to create gouges and scratches. Sandpaper may also be used to soften corners and wear paint off the edges of a finished project.

Double-loading With a double-loaded brush, you can apply two different colors at the same time. Each side of the brush (typically a flat brush) is loaded with a different color, allowing the colors to blend in the center.

Dry brushing This is a method for highlighting or shading a painting using a scant amount of unthinned paint in the brush. Because this technique is hard on brushes, it's best to use an old, worn flat brush.

Enamel A thin, opaque paint which dries to a glossy coat, used especially on porcelain, glass and other slick surfaces.

Fabric paints Fabric paints are made from powder pigments ground in permanent emulsions and binders. These colors will become permanently attached to the fabric fibers. Fabric paints have been grayed down to create subtle color variations. Packaged in jars and squeeze bottles, these paints use water as a solvent.

Faux finish Literally, a false finish. Any technique which uses paint to make a surface such as wood or plastic imitate the appearance of another surface, including marble, woodgrain, textured fabric and verdigris.

Ferrule The metal ring clamped around the bristles in a brush to hold them in place.

Fine-tip applicator A metal or plastic cap, attached to a plastic squeeze bottle of paint, that enables fine linework to be created without the use of a brush.

Flyspecking See Spattering.

Frisket See Masking fluid.

Gel medium Used with acrylic paints to produce transparent effects without thinning the paint consistency.

Gesso A white paste prepared by mixing plaster of paris, gypsum, or another whiting agent with sizing or glue—most often used to prepare a surface such as canvas or linen for painting. Gesso ensures that the oils will not bleed into and rot the fibers of the surface over time.

Glaze A thin, transparent color wash made by mixing water or a thinning medium with acrylic paint or thinner with oil paint.

Highlights Areas of white or lightest color in a painting which represent reflected light.

Hue The quality or intensity of a color—as in a tint or shade.

Hot-pressed The smoothest type of artist's paper, having very little tooth. Good for graphite, pen-and-ink and other drawing methods.

Kneaded eraser A pliable, non-abrasive eraser that can be easily manipulated and used to erase graphite and chalks from a surface. It can also be pressed into an area of color to lift mistakes or create highlights.

Lacquer A finishing varnish which contains mineral spirits which evaporate as the lacquer dries, leaving a glossy coating.

Malachite A painted finish which mimics the intensive pattern of irregular, wavy shapes found in the mineral malachite.

Marbleizing Using paints and brushes (or feathers) to imitate the veined look of marble.

Masking fluid A product used primarily with watercolors which is applied to any areas of a painting the artist wishes to remain white. After the painting is complete, the mask can be rubbed off, revealing the protected areas. Also called frisket.

Matte A non-glossy finish. Matte sprays are aerosol sealants or fixatives that disappear when dry, leaving no sheen on the surface.

Moiré A painted finish that mimics the wavy or watery pattern of *moiré* fabric.

Mopping Lightly brushing color to soften or blend it in a desired direction using a large, soft-bristled mop brush.

Mottling Using natural sea sponges and other rough-textured items to create a textured, spotty effect on paintings or walls. Also known as sponging.

Mud Refers to a mixture containing either too many or incompatible colors, or colors that have been overblended until they become muddy, dull or chalky.

Oil paint A rich, thick, buttery paint made of powdered pigment carried in an oil binder. The traditional painting medium, oil is preferred for its color intensity and transparency. Must be thinned and cleaned up with mineral spirits or turpentine. Available in tube form only, in both artist's and student grades.

Opaque Describes paint coverage thick enough that light will not pass through it.

Open time The period in which paints will remain workable before they begin to "set up" and dry.

Paper bag sanding Using brown paper grocery bags as an extra-fine sandpaper to lightly smooth base coats without roughing up the surface as sandpaper does.

Papier-mâché Literally, chewed or pulped paper. A hard, cardboard-like surface made from layers of paper or paper pulp, water and a binding agent, then modeled into various shapes.

Pickling Applying a white- or light-colored glaze or thinned paint mixture to a wood surface and wiping it off, resulting in a light, transparent finish which allows the wood grain to show through. Similar to staining.

Plate surface Hot-pressed paper that has been made extremely smooth with the addition of a clay or plastic coating.

Ragging Pressing a crumpled rag dipped in paint onto a surface to create texture. A dry rag can also be used to lift wet paint off a surface, thereby creating a "negative" textured finish.

Rag rolling Using a rag crumpled into a cylindrical form to roll color onto a surface. A dry rag can be rolled over wet paint to lift paint off and create a negative texture.

Rosemaling Derived from the Norwegian word *mahling*, meaning painting, rosemaling is the painted decoration of such items as cabinets, trunks and wooden dinnerware in Scandinavian peasant style. Consists especially of floral designs, scrolled patterns and inscriptions. There are several geographical subcategories, such as Hallingdal, Telemark and Rogalund.

Rough papers Similar to cold-press papers, but with a greater degree of tooth, or texture. Used especially for watercolors.

Salt resist Using salt as a textural medium with watercolor paints and silk dyes. When sprinkled onto a wet painting, the granules break up the pigment and pull color toward them, creating a mottled effect.

Sealer A clear liquid protective coat that can be applied prior to any base coating or staining to protect the wood and ensure ease in wiping off mistakes. Applied again once the surface is finished, it seals the paint and protects it from the elements. Sold at most hardware, home improvement and craft stores.

Shade Any color with black added to it. For example, maroon is a shade of red.

Shellac A purified form of lacquer which contains a solvent such as alcohol and is used to finish wood.

Sizing A coating added to paper pulp or applied to the finished surface of paper to control its absorbency and prevent paint from bleeding through its fibers.

Solvent The agent that cleans and thins a particular paint. Turpentine is a solvent for oil paints, while water may be used as a solvent for acrylics.

Spattering Pulling a palette knife or thumb across the bristles of a toothbrush or stencil brush loaded with thinned paint to create a random spray of droplets. Also called flyspecking, this technique is used as a decorative finish, especially for weathered or antiqued objects.

Sponging Using a sponge loaded with paint to apply a textured pattern to a surface. Also known as mottling.

Spouncing Also known as pouncing or stippling. Gently tapping the flattened hairs or sponge-tip of a brush

against a surface, generally using only a scant amount of paint, resulting in a light, slightly textured coverage of paint. Commonly used in stenciling.

Staining Applying and then wiping off a glaze or thinned paint mixture to any wooden surface, thereby bringing out the natural grain of the wood. Usually done with natural brown tones to simulate more expensive wood grains, such as mahogany, cherry or walnut.

Sta-Wet palette Specially treated paper that is soaked, then placed over a wet sponge inside the lidded palette box. Paints squeezed onto the palette paper remain moist, extending open time considerably.

Steel wool Coarse, abrasive pads composed of long, fine steel shavings—sometimes treated with oils—which are used to sand or buff surfaces.

Stippling A texturing technique commonly used in stenciling. Can also be used to create fur and foliage in a painting. Stippling involves pouncing a brush loaded with a scant amount of paint onto a surface until the area is lightly covered.

Strié A finish that features irregular linear streaks created in a wet paint glaze with a flogger brush.

Strokework A methodical, practiced approach to painting wherein designs are created by combining any of a series of recognized brushstrokes such as the comma stroke, broad stroke and S-stroke.

Student grade colors A grade of paints lesser in quality (and thereby less expensive) than artist's grade but can be truer in hue than craft varieties.

Stylus A metal tool with a dull point used to transfer patterns with graphite paper.

Tack cloth A specially treated, slightly sticky cloth used to remove fine dust particles and sanding residue.

Thinner A liquid used to reduce the thickness of a paint. Water is used as a thinner for watercolors and acrylics, turpentine for oils.

Tint Any color with white added to it. For example, pink is a tint of red.

Tole In the traditional sense, tole painting refers only to decorative painting done on tinplate or tinware. Today, the term is used loosely (and erroneously) to refer to any decorative painting on a variety of surfaces.

Tooth The texture or rough quality of a surface, specifically when referring to paper.

Tortoiseshell A *faux* finish mottled with deep browns and golds which imitates the pattern of tortoiseshell.

Tracing paper Thin, slightly transparent paper which can be laid directly over a pattern, allowing the lines underneath to show through so that a copy can be traced.

Transfer paper Thin paper coated on the back with graphite or chalk, used to transfer a design onto any surface by placing the coated side on the surface and tracing over the design with a stylus.

Transparent Describes a coating of paint thin enough to allow light to pass through.

Varnish Any sealant applied to a finished surface to protect it from moisture, scratches and other elements. Water-based varnishes should be used over acrylics and other water-based paints, while oil-based varnish should be used over oil paints.

Vellum Traditionally, a fine parchment paper made from calf or lamb skin. Cold-pressed paper is sometimes referred to as vellum.

Verdigris A green or greenish-blue finish resulting from the aging and oxidization of a copper, brass or bronze surface. This effect can also be created with paint on metal or nonmetal surfaces.

Wash Paint thinned to an ink-like consistency with water or a painting medium, creating a transparent layer of color which adds depth while still allowing the base color to show through.

Wet-into-wet A technique that creates a blended, flowing look by applying paint to an area already covered in wet paint or water. Generally used with water-based mediums, especially watercolors.

Wood graining A painted finish that duplicates the appearance of wood by texturing a wet paint glaze with brushes and specialized wood graining tools, such as a wood graining comb.

PART TWO

SUPPLIES AND RESOURCES

Paints

Most paints are made simply of a combination of binder and pigment. The binder is different depending on the medium, but in most cases, the pigment is the same. Most paints pose no health risks as long as they're used as directed. Always check labels for warnings. When buying paint, ask for a complete color guide to that particular manufacturer's line to help you with pigment selection.

ACRYLIC PAINTS

Accent Country Colors
Koh-I-Noor, Inc.
100 North St.
Bloomsbury, NJ 08804
Tel: (800) 631-7646

Aleene's Premium Coat
Duncan Enterprises, Inc.
5673 E. Shields Ave.
Fresno, CA 93727
Tel: (209) 291-4444

Anita's Acrylic Craft Paint
Back Street, Inc.
3905 Steve Reynolds Blvd.
Norcross, GA 30093
Tel: (800) 228-2319

Cryla Artists' Acrylic Color
Daler-Rowney U.S.A./Robert
Simmons

2 Corporate Dr.
Cranbury, NJ 08512
Tel: (609) 655-5252

Da Vinci Acrylic Colors
Da Vinci Paint Co., Inc.
11 Good Year St.
Irvine, CA 92718
Tel: (714) 859-4890

DecoArt Americana Acrylic Colors
DecoArt
P.O. Box 386
Stanford, KY 40484
Tel: (800) 367-3047

Delta Ceramcoat Colors
Delta Technical Coatings
2550 Pellissier Pl.
Whittier, CA 90601
Tel: (800) 423-4135

FolkArt Acrylic Colors
Plaid Enterprises
P.O. Box 7600
Norcross, GA 30091
Tel: (770) 923-8200

Golden Artist Colors, Inc.
Bell Road
New Berlin, NY 13411
Tel: (607) 847-6154

Holbein Acrylics
HK Holbein, Inc.
20 Commerce St., Box 555
Williston, VT 05495
Tel: (800) 682-6686

Jo Sonja Artists' Colors
Chroma Acrylics, Inc.
205 Bucky Dr.
Lititz, PA 17543
Tel: (717) 626-8866

Liquitex Acrylic Artist Colors
Binney & Smith, Inc.
1100 Church Lane
Easton, PA 18044
Tel: (610) 253-6271

Modern Options
2325 Third Street, No. 339
San Francisco, CA 94107
Tel: (415) 252-5580

Prima Acrylics
Martin/F. Weber Co.
2727 Southampton Road
Philadelphia, PA 19154
Tel: (215) 677-5600

Prism Acrylic Paints
Palmer Paint Products, Inc.
P.O. Box 1058
Troy, MI 48099
Tel: (313) 588-4500

Rembrandt Acrylics
Canson-Talens, Inc.
21 Industrial Drive
P.O. Box 220
South Hadley, MA 01075
Tel: (800) 628-9283

Shiva Acrylics
Creative Art Products Co.
1558 S. Henderson St.
Galesburg, IL 61401
Tel: (800) 945-4535

Winsor & Newton Artists' Acrylic
Colours
Col-Art Americas, Inc.
11 Constitution Ave.
Piscataway, NJ 08855
Tel: (908) 562-0770

OIL PAINTS

Archival Oils
Chroma Acrylics, Inc.
205 Bucky Dr.
Lititz, PA 17543
Tel: (800) 257-8278

Daler-Rowney Artists Oil Colours
Daler-Rowney U.S.A./
Robert Simmons

2 Corporate Dr.
Cranbury, NJ 08512
Tel: (609) 655-5252

Gamblin Artists' Colors
P.O. Box 625
Portland, OR 97207
Tel: (503) 235-1945

Grumbacher Pre-tested Artists' Oil
Colors, Max Grumbacher and
Gainsborough Oils
Koh-I-Noor, Inc.
100 North St.
P.O. Box 68
Bloomsbury, NJ 08804
Tel: (908) 479-4124

Holbein Oils
HK Holbein, Inc.
20 Commerce St., Box 555
Williston, VT 05495
Tel: (800) 682-6686

Liquitex Artist Oil Colors
Binney & Smith, Inc.
1100 Church Lane
Easton, PA 18044
Tel: (610) 253-6271

Permalba Artists' Oil Colors
Martin/F. Weber Co.
2727 Southampton Road
Philadelphia, PA 19154
Tel: (215) 677-5600

Rembrandt Oils
Canson-Talens, Inc.
P.O. Box 220
S. Hadley, MA 01075
Tel: (413) 538-9250

Shiva Signature Oil Colors
Creative Art Products, Inc.
P.O. Box 129
Knoxville, IL 61448
Tel: (309) 342-0179

Winsor & Newton Artists' Oils
Col-Art Americas, Inc.
11 Constitution Ave.
Piscataway, NJ 08855
Tel: (908) 562-0770

Yarka/Fostport, Inc.
65 Eastern Ave.
Essex, MA 01929
Tel: (508) 768-3350

WATERCOLORS

Daler-Rowney Artists' Watercolours
Daler-Rowney U.S.A./
Robert Simmons
2 Corporate Dr.
Cranbury, NJ 08512
Tel: (609) 655-5252

Fantasia Watercolors
Sakura of America
30780 San Clemente Street
Hayward, CA 94544
Tel: (800) 776-6257

Grumbacher Academy Watercolors
Koh-I-Noor, Inc.
100 North St.
Bloomsbury, NJ 08804
Tel: (800) 631-7646

Holbein Watercolors
HK Holbein, Inc.
20 Commerce St., Box 555
Williston, VT 05495
Tel: (800) 682-6686

Liquitex Watercolors
Binney & Smith, Inc.
1100 Church Lane
Easton, PA 18044
Tel: (610) 253-6271

Permalba Watercolors
Martin/F Weber Co.
2727 Southampton Rd.
Philadelphia, PA 19154
Tel: (215) 677-5600

Rembrandt Watercolors
Canson-Talens, Inc.
21 Industrial Drive
P.O. Box 220
South Hadley, MA 01075
Tel: (800) 628-9283

Winsor & Newton Artists'
Watercolours
Col-Art Americas, Inc.
11 Constitution Ave.
Piscataway, NJ 08855
Tel: (908) 562-0770

Yarka/Fostport, Inc.
65 Eastern Ave.
Essex, MA 01929
Tel: (508) 768-3350

ALKYDS

Grumbacher
Koh-I-Noor, Inc.
100 North St.
P.O. Box 68
Bloomsbury, NJ 08804
Tel: (800) 631-7646

Winsor & Newton's Griffin Alkyd
Colors
Col-Art Americas, Inc.
11 Constitution Ave.
P.O. Box 1396
Piscataway, NJ 08855
Tel: (908) 562-0770

Decorative Painter's Guide to Brushes

Making a trip to the art-supply store for brushes can be a bewildering experience. The choices are innumerable and knowing which brushes you need can be a real guessing game. To help you make more informed buying decisions, we've compiled a few facts about brushes.

CHOOSING A BRUSH

First of all, keep in mind that every brush is made to manipulate one of two kinds of paint: fluid, free-flowing paint or thick, viscous paint. The fluid paints include watercolors, acrylics and oils that are thinned down to a free-flowing state. A viscous paint (either oil or acrylic) is one that's used straight from the tube or jar, and is thus very thick.

Let's begin by taking a look at the specific characteristics a brush must have for fluid media:

• The brush must hold a good point or edge when wet. Combatting a brush that's constantly splitting or fraying when you load it with color is a no-win situation.
• The brush must have good spring or "snap." This means that the brush bounces back to its original shape when you lift it from the painting surface after a stroke. Without this spring, you waste a lot of energy shaping the brush and trying to get it to give a consistent stroke of color.
• Most important, the brush must offer consistent flow of color from the brush tip. Flow control is the most critical ingredient in a good brush. Flow control means that paint of the same thickness will flow from the brush tip at the same rate every time it hits the painting surface.

NATURAL VS. SYNTHETIC

Brushes made from Kolinsky Sable are considered to be the best. They also require a run to the bank for the larger sizes. Lesser grade sable hair also makes for a good, functional brush. And there are other natural hairs that offer varying degrees of performance.

• Squirrel-hair brushes offer terrific flow control and form a good point, but don't have the degree of snap that a sable brush does. Squirrel hair makes for great flat and wash brushes.
• Sabeline brushes can be an economical alternative to sable. The hairs from this brush are taken from the ox and are bleached and dyed to resemble sable. They have reasonable flow control and moderate point and spring, making for good flat brushes.
• Pony has reasonable flow control, but poor spring and point.
• Camel, contrary to its name, is a catch-all term for brushes that are made from a variety of lower-quality hairs.

Brushes made from synthetic filaments can be a nice, economical alternative to natural-hair brushes. Nylon brushes are excellent for media that aren't completely free-flowing, such as acrylic.

Because nylon filaments are glass-smooth, they don't have the degree of flow control necessary for paints as fluid as watercolor. Recently, however, brushes have come to the market using polyester and these are better suited for use with watercolor. They also have great snap and point at an affordable price.

If you're using thick color right out of the jar or tube, you'll need a stiff brush such as one made from hog bristle. The best hog-bristle brushes use bristle that interlocks or curves inward slightly. The best bristle "flags" or has split ends to give you control over thicker colors.

ABOUT SIZES

How brushes are labeled numerically for size will vary by manufacturer, country of origin and use. In general, low numbers are smaller. Fluid-media round brushes are labeled for size starting at teeny-tiny with "10/0." The brushes get larger up through size "5/0" (pretty tiny) to "0" (small). The brushes then increase in size with numerals up to 20 or 24. Bristle rounds and flats are usually sized starting at 1 and will range up to 20 or 24. The same number in a bristle brush will denote a larger size than in a soft, fluid-media brush. Within a series, brushes are usually numbered in size according to the width or diameter of the body of hairs at the ferrule.

The length of the hairs in a brush must be taken into consideration, also. Shorter hairs are excellent for detail strokes. Longer hairs are better suited to painting long, flowing lines. Generally, longer hairs are more flexible, and hence more difficult to control.

A good all-purpose selection might include a small- to medium-size round and flat, a larger round and flat, a liner, and perhaps a fan for blending. Once you've become comfortable with these, you can decide which of the other brushes you want to add to your paint box.

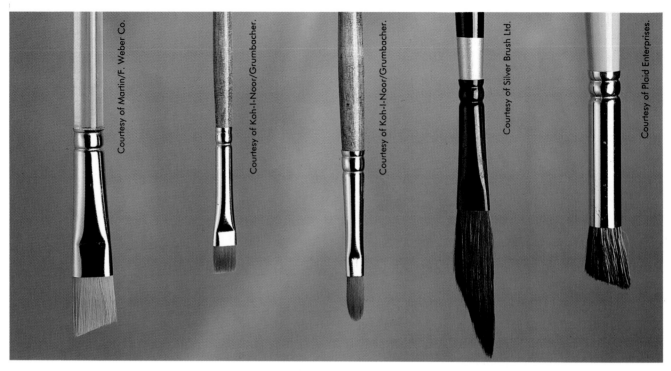

Courtesy of Martin/F. Weber Co.

Courtesy of Koh-I-Noor/Grumbacher.

Courtesy of Koh-I-Noor/Grumbacher.

Courtesy of Silver Brush Ltd.

Courtesy of Plaid Enterprises.

Angular　　*Bright/Chisel Blender*　　*Cat's Tongue*　　*Dagger/Striper*　　*Deerfoot Stippler*

ANGULAR

The angular brush is capable of many different painting feats. Its shape allows you to create softly shaded areas, even in tight spots. It's often used to create the strokes that form roses, because of the contrasts created between sharply defined edges and contrasting soft areas.

In addition to roses, you can also take advantage of this brush's sharp point to work in the leaves. Then use it to fill in color and blend. A small angular brush could be used to shade tight areas, such as the dark areas of these berries and their shadows.

BRIGHT/CHISEL BLENDER

The short, compact hairs of the bright (which looks like a flat with shorter bristles) are perfect for creating controlled strokes and doing precision blending as on these cherries. This brush performs especially well with heavy mediums.

CAT'S TONGUE

The rounded corners of this brush make it useful for filling in areas of color and working with control in crowded areas of a painting. With oils, it's often used to soften or lose edges, blending one color into another without losing the definition of shape. Some basic strokes, such as those at right, can also be made with the cat's tongue.

DAGGER/STRIPER

The striper can create long strokes of varied widths, so it's ideal for painting lines, borders, ribbons, foliage and vines. The chiseled edge is suitable for drawing lines, and the thickness of the brush allows lengthy strokework without reloading.

Load it fully with paint to create long, uninterrupted ribbons.

DEERFOOT STIPPLER

The stippler is a popular brush among decorative artists because of the wide range of texturizing techniques for which you can use it. When dry, the stippler can be used to paint foliage, such as this tree, using the pouncing technique. To paint long fur, drag the brush toward you. Drag the brush away from you to paint grasses.

Fan   ***Flat Shader***   ***Oval Wash***   ***One Stroke***   ***Grass Comb***   ***Long Liner/ Script***

FAN

The fan is another popular brush. It's most often used to create trees, shrubbery and grasses. It's also useful for blending and softening the edges of other strokes where a smooth look is desired.

Use the fan to softly blend and drag colors, as in these clouds. While the paint is still workable, sweep over the painted clouds with the fan brush to drag and soften the colors.

Palm trees can be suggested quickly with the fan brush. Use wet paint for this soft effect or drier paint to show individual leaves. (The trunk is painted by stacking pairs of strokes with a flat shader.)

LONG LINER/SCRIPT

The long liner carries more paint than the short liner. Since this thin brush doesn't require frequent loading, it's suitable for forming long, flowing strokes, graceful scrolls and meandering tendrils, such as those below.

GRASS COMB

This texturizing brush makes detailing less time-consuming. It's perfect for painting fur and hair using several layers of different colors. It also makes a quick job of painting grasses. You can use it to create texture, such as that of old, weathered wood, and for cross-hatching.

OVAL WASH

The oval wash, like other wash brushes, is good for laying down color softly with broad, sweeping strokes. It also works well for detail work because it allows you to paint close to areas you've already painted with an accuracy that rivals the tapered end of the round brush.

The oval wash can also create unique effects for border designs. The examples above show the result of a wet brush (top), a medium-wet brush (middle) and a drier brush (bottom).

FLAT SHADER

This brush has a fine, chiseled edge that allows you to create strokes like the S-stroke, crescent, scroll and leaf. As at right, the brush can also be used to block in large areas of flat color, can be side loaded to create modulated color or can be double-loaded to create highlights and shading.

ONE-STROKE

The hairs of the one-stroke are arranged flat but are longer than the shader. It's suitable for lettering work, and painting lines and borders, because the brush can easily create varied line widths depending on the amount of pressure you place on it and whether you use the chisel edge. This brush makes painting checkerboard squares a snap. It's also ideal for painting bricks.

MOP

The soft, fluffy mop brush is a blending and softening brush. It's intended to be used over wet colors to blur edges slightly. It's great for softening edges when doing antiquing and glazing work.

Stroking several times with a mop brush, moving freely in all directions, will soften the edge of a wet glaze application, fading it into the background. In this sample painting, the right side of the handle shows how the project looked just after antiquing, before "dusting" with the mop. On the left, it has been blended. In between, the original background color is shown.

SCRUBBER (Fabric)

The tapered round scrubber is a sturdy bristled brush that is made to withstand scrubbing and stenciling on fabric and other tough surfaces.

SHORT LINER

When loaded with thinned paint, the short liner is well suited for monogramming, highlighting (as on the facial features at right), outlining and strokework.

ROUND

The round brush is well suited for strokework because, like the liner, it can hold enough paint for long, flowing lines and borders. Its point can also be used for detail work in tight areas.

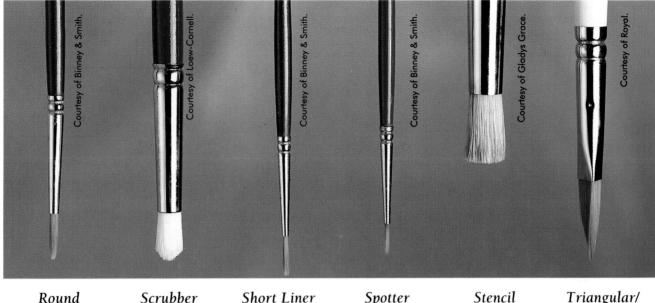

| *Round* | *Scrubber* | *Short Liner* | *Spotter* | *Stencil* | *Triangular/ Wedge* |

SPOTTER

The spotter's few, short hairs meet at a tiny point. With it, you can paint highlights and tiny details (such as eyelashes, eyebrows and eye highlights) and work in hard-to-reach areas with a great deal of control.

STENCIL

The stencil brush is made with soft but sturdy bristles to withstand the pounding it receives from stenciling techniques. Paint should be loaded into the stencil brush lightly, so when tapped gently on the back of your hand, no paint appears. If you paint with several colors, be sure to use a different brush for each color.

Stencil brushes aren't limited to stenciling, however. If you have difficulty painting cheeks without hard edges, try a small stencil brush. You can also buff subtle colors or value changes onto solid backgrounds to create interest.

TRIANGULAR/WEDGE

The triangular brush can be loaded on three sides to create ribbons, leaves, petals and more. The tapered, long point produces a thin, graceful end on brushstrokes and decorative detail work. It's a fun brush for experimenting. For ribbons, try changing the application of pressure and double loading for variety.

Brushes, Palettes and Other Tools

BRUSH SUPPLIERS

Whether you're a beginning or advanced painter, your paintbrush is your most important tool. The selection of brushes available to the decorative painter is extensive. Brushes can be made with natural hair, such as kolinsky or red sable, or from synthetic materials, such as nylon or polyester, or a blend of the two. Brushes also come in a variety of shapes and sizes. There are flat and angular brushes, brights, mops, fans, liners and more—each offering a specific quality which makes it best suited for certain strokes and techniques.

Bette Byrd Brushes
P.O. Box 2526
Duluth, GA 30136
Tel: (770) 623-6097
Natural and synthetic hair brushes for oils, acrylics and watercolors.

Binney & Smith, Inc.
1100 Church Lane
Easton, PA 18044
Tel: (610) 253-6271
A full line of natural and synthetic hair brushes for all media.

Creative Art Products Co.
1558 S. Henderson St.

Galesburg, IL 61401
Tel: (800) 945-4535
A selection of brushes for a variety of media.

Daler-Rowney U.S.A./Robert Simmons
2 Corporate Dr.
Cranbury, NJ 08512
Tel: (609) 655-5252
A complete line of natural and synthetic hair brushes for fine artists, tole and decorative painters, and hobbyists.

Da Vinci Paint Co., Inc.
11 Good Year Road
Tarpon Springs, FL 34689
Tel: (800) 334-3683
A variety of artists' brushes for different media.

Demco Industries, Inc.
P.O. Box 1459
52 Mason Road
Champlain, NY 12919
Tel: (800) 336-7516
A selection of brushes for various media.

Dove Brushes
280 Terrace Road
Tarpon Springs, FL 34689
Tel: (800) 334-3683
A wide selection of brushes from shaders to liners.

F.M. Brush Co., Inc.
70-02 72nd Place
Glendale, NY 11385
Tel: (718) 821-5939
Offers a full line of artists' brushes.

HK Holbein, Inc.
20 Commerce St., Box 555
Williston, VT 05495
Tel: (800) 682-6686
A selection of brushes for a variety of media.

Grumbacher/Accent
Koh-I-Noor, Inc.
100 North St.
Bloomsbury, NJ 08804
Tel: (800) 631-7646
A complete line of brushes for oils, acrylics and watercolors.

Jack Richeson & Co., Inc.
557 Marcella Dr.
Kimberly, WI 54126
Tel: (800) 233-2404
A selection of brushes for acrylics, watercolors and oils.

Loew-Cornell, Inc.
563 Chestnut Ave.
Teaneck, NJ 07666
Tel: (201) 836-7070
Natural and synthetic hair brushes

for fine arts, decorative painting, fabric crafts and *faux* finishing.

Martin/F. Weber, Inc.
2727 Southampton Road
Philadelphia, PA 19154
Tel: (215) 677-5600
A variety of brushes for the decorative painter.

Marx Brush Inc.
130 Beckwith Ave.
Paterson, NJ 07503
Tel: (800) 654-6279
A variety of brushes for fabric painting, hobbies, crafts, tole and decorative painting.

Plaid Enterprises
P.O. Box 7600
Norcross, GA 30091
Tel: (770) 923-8200
A variety of brushes for the decorative painter.

Raphael & Berge
In U.S.A. Sosh Sales
216 East Navarre St.
South Bend, IN 46601
Tel: (219) 232-5819
A selection of fine art and craft brushes for a variety of media.

Royal Brush Manufacturing Co.
6949 Kennedy Ave.

Hammond, IN 46323
Tel: (800) 247-2211
A full line of brushes for a variety of media.

Silver Brush Limited
5 Oxford Court
Princeton Junction, NJ 08550
Tel: (609) 275-8691
A full range of brushes to suit all techniques and media.

Winsor & Newton
Col-Art Americas, Inc.
11 Constitution Ave.
Piscataway, NJ 08855
Tel: (908) 562-0770
A full line of brushes for oils, acrylics, watercolors, tole and decorative painting.

Yarka/Fostport, Inc.
65 Eastern Ave.
Essex, MA 01929
Tel: (508) 768-3350
A full line of brushes for oils, acrylics and watercolors.

Yasutomo and Co.
490 Eccles Ave.
So. San Francisco, CA 94080
Tel: (415) 737-8888
A selection of decorative painting and craft brushes.

OTHER TOOLS

Some other helpful tools for the decorative painter:

Daler-Rowney U.S.A./
Robert Simmons
2 Corporate Dr.
Cranbury, NJ 08512
Tel: (609) 655-5252
Lidded palette for acrylics.

Kemper Enterprises, Inc.
13595 12th St.
Chino, CA 91710
Tel: (909) 627-6191
Spattering brush (for flyspecking), fluid writer pen (for trimming) and a wipe-out tool (for correcting mistakes).

Masterson Sta-Wet Palette
Masterson Art Products, Inc.
P.O. Box 10775
Glendale, AZ 85318
Tel: (602) 263-6017
Sta-Wet palette (an airtight palette box to keep acrylic paints fresh longer).

Saral Paper Co., Inc.
322 W. 57th St., Suite 30T
New York, NY 10019
Tel: (212) 247-0460
Transferring paper in several colors.

Brush Cleaners

How long a brush will last depends partially on the quality of your new brush, but proper care and maintenance are just as important. Store brushes upright in a container or lay them flat, but never rest a brush on its hairs. Be sure to clean your brushes during a painting session for fast-drying paints like acrylics. Clean your brushes *after* every painting session no matter the medium. Many artists clean their brushes with a solvent and soap and water alone, but many manufacturers offer cleaners specifically designed for cleaning brushes of oils or acrylics.

Accent
Koh-I-Noor, Inc.
100 North St.
Bloomsbury, NJ 08804
Tel: (800) 631-7646

Alvin & Company
1335 Blue Hills Ave. Ext.
Bloomfield, CT 06002
Tel: (800) 444-2584

Da Vinci Paint Co., Inc.
11 Good Year St.
Irvine, CA 92718
Tel: (714) 859-4890

General Pencil Co.
67-73 Fleet St.
Jersey City, NJ 07306
Tel: (201) 653-5351

Loew-Cornell, Inc.
563 Chestnut Ave.
Teaneck, NJ 07666
Tel: (201) 836-7070

Martin/F. Weber Co.
2727 Southampton Road
Philadelphia, PA 19154
Tel: (215) 677-5600

Marx Brush Inc.
130 Beckwith Ave.
Paterson, NJ 07503
Tel: (800) 654-6279

Raphael & Berge
In U.S.A. Sosh Sales
216 East Navarre St.
South Bend, IN 46601
Tel: (219) 232-5819

Silver Brush Ltd.
5 Oxford Court
Princeton Junction, NJ 08550
Tel: (609) 275-8691

Winsor & Newton
Col-Art Americas, Inc.
11 Constitution Ave.
Piscataway, NJ 08855
Tel: (908) 562-0770

Sealers and Varnishes

Proper preparation of a surface is crucial to successful decorative painting. And, once your painting is complete and dry, a varnish will protect the painting from dirt and oils that can be left behind when a piece is handled.

Accent
Koh-I-Noor, Inc.
100 North St.
Bloomsbury, NJ 08804
Tel: (800) 631-7646

Anita's
Back Street, Inc.
3905 Steve Reynolds Blvd.
Norcross, GA 30093
Tel: (800) 228-2319

Ceramcoat
Delta Technical Coatings
2550 Pellissier Pl.
Whittier, CA 90601
Tel: (800) 423-4135

Daler-Rowney U.S.A./Robert Simmons
2 Corporate Dr.
Cranbury, NJ 08512
Tel: (609) 655-5252

FolkArt
Plaid Enterprises
P.O. Box 7600
Norcross, GA 30091
Tel: (770) 923-8200

Jo Sonja's
Chroma Acrylics, Inc.
205 Bucky Dr.
Lititz, PA 17543
Tel: (717) 626-8866

Krylon
Krlon/The Specialty Division
31500 Solon Road
Solon, OH 44139
Tel: (800) 797-3332

Right-Step/First Step
J.W. Etc. Quality Products
2205 First St., Suite 103
Simi Valley, CA 93065
Tel: (805) 526-5066

Faux Finishing Supplies

Whether used alone or combined with decorative painting, *faux* finishing techniques, such as marbleizing, sponging, antiquing and crackling, add distinctive effects to everything from furniture and walls to smaller pieces like wooden boxes.

Back Street, Inc.
3905 Steve Reynolds Blvd.
Norcross, GA 30093
Tel: (800) 228-2319
Faux Easy Glazes and other products for an assortment of *faux* finishing techniques.

B.D. Classics
P.O. Box 2445
Santa Fe Springs, CA 90670
Tel: (800) 543-8551
Kits for marbleizing in a variety of real marble colors.

Daler-Rowney U.S.A./Robert Simmons
2 Corporate Dr.
Cranbury, NJ 08512

Tel: (609) 655-5252
Goldfinger gold-leafing materials.

DecoArt
P.O. Box 386
Stanford, KY 40484
Tel: (800) 367-3047
A range of products for such techniques as crackling and sponging.

Delta Technical Coatings
2550 Pellissier Place
Whittier, CA 90601
Tel: (800) 423-4135
Wood stains, pickling and antiquing gels, and foiling kits.

FolkArt
Plaid Enterprises
P.O. Box 7600
Norcross, GA 30091
Tel: (404) 923-8200
Antiquing and crackling mediums, pickling stains and patina solutions.

Golden Artist Colors, Inc.
Bell Road

New Berlin, NY 13411
Tel: (607) 847-6154
A line of decorative finishing kits and custom finishing colors.

Koh-I-Noor, Inc.
100 North St.
P.O. Box 68
Bloomsbury, NJ 08804
Tel: (800) 631-7646
Water-based decorating glazes for a variety of finishing techniques.

Modern Options
2325 Third St., No. 339
San Francisco, CA 94107
Tel: (415) 252-5580
Finishing kits and antiquing solutions.

Palmer Paint Products, Inc.
1291 Rochester Road
Troy, MI 48083
Tel: (800) 521-1383
Products and kits for finishes such as verdigris.

Stencils and Stenciling Products

Whether you're using pre-cut stencils or cutting your own, the stenciling technique is a fast and easy way to add a beautiful hand-painted look to walls, furniture, floors and an endless number of other surfaces.

Accent
Koh-I-Noor, Inc.
100 North St.
Bloomsbury, NJ 08804
Tel: (800) 631-7646

American Traditional Stencils
Rt. 4, Box 519
Northwood, NH 03261
Tel: (603) 942-8100

Back Street, Inc.
3905 Steve Reynolds Blvd.
Norcross, GA 30093
Tel: (800) 228-2319
Rubber press stencils and paints.

Buckingham Stencils, Inc.
1574 Gulf Road, Suite 1107
Point Roberts, WA 98281
Tel: (800) 742-8168
Several lines of original stencils and stencil borders.

DecoArt
P.O. Box 386
Stanford, KY 40484
Tel: (800) 367-3047
Stencil paints in a range of colors.

Delta Technical Coatings
2550 Pellissier Pl.
Whittier, CA 90601
Tel: (800) 423-4135
A line of stencils and stencil paint creme in a variety of colors.

Glady's Grace, Inc.
213 Killingly Rd.
Pomfret Center, CT 06259
Tel: (203) 928-2034
A line of originally designed stencils.

Loew-Cornell, Inc.
563 Chestnut Ave.
Teaneck, NJ 07666
Tel: (201) 836-7070

MB Historic Decor
P.O. Box 880
Norwich, VT 05055
Tel: (802) 649-1790
A line of early New England stencils.

one heart . . . one mind
310 N. Second St. E.
Rexburg, ID 83440
Tel: (208) 356-3690
A selection of stencils and stenciling tools.

Plaid Enterprises
P.O. Box 7600
Norcross, GA 30091
Tel: (404) 923-8200

Royal Design Studio
386 E 'H' St., Suite 209-188
Chula Vista, CA 91910
Tel: (619) 482-5671
An extensive selection of original stencils.

Saral Paper Co., Inc.
322 W. 57th St., Suite 30T
New York, NY 10019
Tel: (212) 247-0460

Stencillusions
V. & Olga Decorating Co.
159 Beach 123 St.
Rockaway Park, NY 11694
Tel: (718) 634-4415
A selection of original stenciling designs.

Fabric Decorating Supplies

Fabric painters have an extensive variety of paints to choose from. In addition to the numerous colors available, there are also glitter paints, metallic paints, pearlescent paints—even glow-in-the-dark paints—which can be used to decorate everything from T-shirts and sweatshirts to table linens and drapes.

Accent
Koh-I-Noor, Inc.
100 North St.
Bloomsbury, NJ 08804
Tel: (908) 479-4124
Fabric paints and dyes in a range of colors.

Daler-Rowney U.S.A./Robert
Simmons
2 Corporate Dr.
Cranbury, NJ 08512
Tel: (609) 655-5252
Pearlescent liquid colors.

DecoArt
P.O. Box 386
Stanford, KY 40484

Tel: (800) 367-3047
Acrylic and dimensional paint for fabrics.

Deka
Decart/Deka, Inc.
P.O. Box 309
Morrisville, VT 05661
Tel: (802) 888-4217
Silk and fabric paints in a full range of colors.

Delta Technical Coatings
2550 Pellissier Place
Whittier, CA 90601
Tel: (800) 423-4135
A line of fabric paints, dyes and other embellishments.

Duncan Enterprises, Inc.
5673 E. Shields Ave.
Fresno, CA 93727
Tel: (209) 291-4444
A variety of fabric paints and other accents.

Jacquard
Rupert, Gibbon & Spider, Inc.

P.O. Box 425
Healdsburg, CA 95448
Tel: (800) 442-0455
Silk and textile colors.

Liquitex
Binney & Smith, Inc.
1100 Church Lane
Easton, PA 18044
Tel: (610) 253-6271
Glitter and opalescent paints.

Plaid Enterprises
P.O. Box 7600
Norcross, GA 30091
Tel: (404) 923-8200
A wide selection of fabric paints and other embellishments.

Tulip
Polymerics, Inc.
24 Prime Park Way
Natick, MA 01760
Tel: (508) 650-5400
A selection of fabric, metallic and glitter paints.

Decorative painting is unique in its decoration of a functional surface rather than a flat, blank canvas. From wood trays to ceramic pitchers, old tables to table linens, the painting possibilities are endless. Many magazine articles, books and pattern packets include information for obtaining surfaces. You can also find surfaces at decorative painting and craft shops. Flea markets and garage sales are also great places to find surfaces ready for recycling. The following are sources you may also want to contact for some common surfaces.

PAPERS

Arches
Canson-Talens, Inc.
P.O. Box 220
21 Industrial Dr.
So. Hadley, MA 01075
Tel: (413) 538-9250

Canford Paper
Daler-Rowney U.S.A./Robert Simmons
2 Corporate Dr.
Cranbury, NJ 08512
Tel: (609) 655-5252

Lana
Savoire-Faire
P.O. Box 2021
Sausalito, CA 94966
Tel: (800) 332-4660

Strathmore Paper Co.
39 South Broad St.
Westfield, MA 01085
Tel: (413) 568-4827

Yuemei (Handmade Papers)
Eastern Arts Connection
38 Pine Drive
Farmington, CT 06085
Tel: (860) 673-6243

PAPIER-MÂCHÉ

American Art Clay Co., Inc.
4747 West 16th Street
Indianapolis, IN 46222
Tel: (800) 374-1600

Creative Paperclay Co., Inc.
Suite 907
1800 S. Robertson Blvd.
Los Angeles, CA 90035
Tel: (310) 839-0466

Decorator & Craft Corp.
428 S. Zelta
Wichita, KS 67207
Tel: (316) 685-7606

Eastern Arts Connection
38 Pine Drive
Farmington, CT 06085
Tel: (860) 673-6243

WOOD

This list provides a small sampling of the wide variety of wood surfaces available to the decorative artist. Look for products manufactured by the companies listed as wholesale or retail in your local craft and hobby stores, or call for more information on locations in your area. Companies which offer direct sales will sell directly to the consumer via trade shows or mail order.

Allen's Wood Crafts
Route 3
3020 Dogwood Lane
Sapulpa, OK 74066
(918) 224-8796
"Useful items" such as trunks and boxes. No cutouts. All items made from white pine. Wholesale to shops, retail/direct at trade shows. Catalog is $3.50. No minimum order is required, and credit cards are accepted.

Bayer Wood Products
5139 Dorr St.
Toledo, OH 43615
(800) 323-0817
Lots of basic country cutouts as well as a wide selection of finials, dowels, boxes, hearts and beads. Wholesale. Retail sales at shop in Toledo only. Free catalog. Three credit references required to open an account. No minimum wholesale purchase required. Credit cards accepted. Special orders accepted if prepaid or COD.

Bear Creek Woodworks
250 Broadway St.
P.O. Box 362
Quincy, IL 62306
(800) 373-6158
Classic surfaces such as shelves, peg racks and benches with a definite country feel. Wholesale to shops, retail/direct at trade shows. Catalog is $3. New accounts are opened with three credit references. Orders are shipped within 15 days.

Bridgewater Scrollworks
Route 1, Box 585
Osage, MN 56570
(218) 573-3094
Many of the pine and birch pieces offered are original designs. Offers unique products such as nativity scenes and rocking horse bookends. Will custom-cut wood pieces. Wholesale/retail/direct. Catalog is $5, price redeemable with purchase of $10 or more. Credit card orders accepted. No minimum order required. Items priced by quantity.

Cabin Craft Southwest
1500 Westpark Way
Euless, TX 76040
(800) 877-1515
Wide variety of wood pieces, from cutouts to cabinets and stools. Wholesale/retail/direct (call for retail requirements). Catalog is $4. All orders shipped UPS. $100 minimum purchase for first-time wholesale orders.

Cape Cod Cooperage
1150 Queen Ann Road
East Harwich, MA 02645
(508) 432-0788
Specializing in old-time barrel staves. Custom orders welcome. Wholesale/direct. No catalogs. Credit cards accepted. No minimum purchase required. Items shipped UPS.

Casey's Wood Products, Inc.
P.O. Box 365-DA
Woolwich, ME 04579
(800) 45-CASEY
Hearts, balls, eggs, wood turnings, pegs and novelties. Catalog is $1.

Cupboard Distributing
P.O. Box 148
Urbana, OH 43078
(800) 338-6388
Standard wood pieces and wooden jewelry such as scarf clips, pins, bracelets and necklace kits. Wholesale/retail/direct. Catalog is $2. Credit cards accepted. Orders over $100 are shipped free through UPS in continental U.S.

Custom Wood Cut-Outs Unlimited
P.O. Box 518
Massillon, OH 44648
(216) 832-2919
Large variety of cutouts and jewelry. Will custom-cut pieces to order. Retail/direct. Catalog is $2, refundable with first order. No minimum orders required. Check or COD accepted. Volume discounts provided. Items shipped UPS.

Designs by Bentwood, Inc.
170 Big Star Drive
P.O. Box 1676
Thomasville, GA 31792
(912) 226-1223
Classic boxes, buckets, baskets and other containers. All handmade. Retail/direct. Free catalog. No credit card orders. No COD to Canada.

Dick Blick Arts & Crafts
(800) 447-8192 (credit card orders)
(800) 373-7575
Small line of quality wood surfaces, such as standard plaques and sign boards, framed slate boards, mallard ducks and cutouts. Retail only. Free catalog. Credit card orders accepted. Minimum on charge orders is $10. Minimum for shipping is $2.

Drake Distributors
P.O. Box 69
Cottondale, AL 35453
(800) 888-8653
Sprucewood items such as churns, fire screens and chests. Wholesale. Retail showroom in Cottondale. Catalog is $2, $50 minimum purchase for first-time orders.

Duckwork's Woodcrafts
Dept. DA, 7736 Ranchview Lane
Maple Grove, MN 55311
Discount wooden parts. Catalog is $2.

Hofcraft
P.O. Box 72
Grand Haven, MI 49417
(800) 828-0359
Expanded line of boxes, trays, shelves, etc. Most are handcrafted. Wholesale/retail/direct. Catalog is $3 and lists retail prices; however, discounts are given for bulk purchases. No minimum purchase. Credit cards accepted. Most orders shipped within 24 hours. Special orders considered.

Hollins Enterprises, Inc.
P.O. Box 148
670 Orchard Lane
Alpha, OH 45301
(800) 543-3465
Plaques, tavern signs, cutouts, seasonal and holiday wood surfaces. Wholesale/retail/direct via mail order and showroom. Catalog is $5. Minimum first-time order is $100; $30 minimum for reorders. Credit cards and COD accepted. Orders filled within 48 hours.

Johnson's Wood-n-Things
S. 45 W. 33472 Hengen Drive
Dousman, WI 53118
(414) 392-2189
Small but unique selection of products—such as a flag balancer and an antique horse—featured in many painting books and magazines. Custom orders welcome. Retail/direct. Catalog is free with a business-size SASE. Orders are shipped within 3-5 days. Charge on shipping is 15%.

Mill Store Products
P.O. Box 40716
39 South St.
New Bedford, MA 02744
(800) 444-7772
White pine or other hardwood pieces, including large-size cutouts for outdoor use, as well as planters of many shapes and sizes. Wholesale. Catalog is $5, refundable with first order. No credit card orders.

Ornaments Unlimited (Positively Country)
W. 190 S. 7416 Bay Shore Dr.
Muskego, WI 53150
(800) 762-3556
(414) 789-0777 (local calls)
Unfinished wood items featured in painting project books. Custom orders accepted; they do all their own cutting. Wholesale/retail/direct. Catalog is $2; $50 minimum wholesale orders. Most orders shipped within one week.

Rainbow Woods
20 Andrews St.
Newnan, GA 30263
Hardwood turnings such as dowels, candle cups, hearts, eggs, Shaker pegs, napkin rings, boxes, knobs and spindles. Free catalog.

Sechtem's Wood
533 Margaret St.
Russell, KS 67665
(913) 483-2912
Wide variety of wooden boxes. Retail/wholesale/direct. Catalog is $3. Mastercard and Visa accepted.

Stan Brown's Arts & Crafts
13435 NE Whitaker Way
Portland, OR 97230
(800) 547-5531
Boxes, primitive cutouts, country plaques, Shaker pegs, candle cups, etc. Wholesale/retail/direct. Catalog is $5 to consumers, free to retail stores. Visa and MasterCard accepted. Minimum wholesale order is $50. Consumer minimum order is $25.

Viking Woodcrafts Inc.
1317 8th St. SE
Waseca, MN 56093
(507) 835-8043
Extensive selection of wood surfaces. Catalog indicates type of wood used for each item. Wholesale. (Direct only to individuals who cannot locate items at retail outlets.) Credit cards accepted. Catalog is $10.

Walnut Hollow Farm
Rt. 2
Dodgeville, WI 53533
Extensive array of wood items, from birdhouses and clocks to furniture and seasonal surfaces. Contact the company for information and free catalog. No minimum order is required.

Western Woodworks
1142 Olive Branch Lane
San Jose, CA 95120
(408) 997-2356
All products made from native American hardwoods, featuring hurricane lamp bases and more. Visa and MasterCard accepted. Free catalog.

Weston Bowl Mill
714 Main
P.O. Box 218
Weston, VT 05161
(802) 824-6219
A variety of finished and unfinished surfaces, including octagonal rail Susans (a variation of the traditional lazy Susan) and wooden bowls. Retail/wholesale/direct. Catalog is $1. Minimum order is $5 retail, $50 wholesale. Minimum credit card order is $20.

Zim's
P.O. Box 57620
Salt Lake City, UT 84157-0620
(801) 268-2505
Southwestern products, standard small wood pieces, shelves, boxes, baskets and cutouts. Wholesale/retail/direct. Catalog is $10. Credit cards accepted for retail orders only. Wholesale requires minimum quantity and $100 minimum purchase. Orders shipped UPS.

TIN

Bob Reuss
209 Summit St.
Norwich, CT 06360
Tel: (203) 886-7365

Tin Originals, Inc.
P.O. Box 64037
Fayetteville, NC 28306
Tel: (910) 424-1400
Wholesale orders only.
Call for your nearest retail
distributor.

Tolin' Station
P.O. Box 8206
Greensboro, NC 27419
Tel: (910) 855-8932

CANVAS/SILKS/FABRICS

The Bag Lady
P.O. Box 531
West Stockbridge, MA 01266
Tel: (413) 637-3534
Canvas tote bags, aprons and more.

Bag Works
3933 California Pkwy. East
Ft. Worth, TX 76119
Tel: (800) 365-7423
Floor cloths, pillow covers and
more.

Qualin International, Inc.
749 Monterey Blvd.
San Francisco, CA 94127
Tel: (415) 333-8500
Fabric decorative supplies.

Rupert, Gibbon & Spider, Inc.
P.O. Box 425
Healdsburg, CA 95448
Tel: (800) 442-0455
Natural fabrics for surface design.

Tara Materials, Inc.
111 Fredrix Alley
Lawrenceville, GA 30246
Tel: (770) 963-5256
Stretched canvas, canvas panels,
banners and place mats.

GOURDS

Homestead Designs
2826 Old St. Rd. 67 W.
Martinsville, IN 46151
Tel: (317) 342-8097

PORCELAIN

The Gatsonian Detail
Rt. 2, Box 48
Chillicothe, MO 64601

Porcelain By Marilyn
3687 West US 40
Greenfield, IN 46140

RESIN

Design Americana/Design Craft
110-A W. Caston St.
Heath Springs, SC 29058

ETI/Environmental Technology, Inc.
South Bay Depot Road
Fields Landing, CA 95537

Jennings Decoy Co.
601 Franklin Ave. N.E.
St. Cloud, MN 56304
Tel: (800) 331-5613

WORKSHOP CHECKLISTS

Attending a painting workshop is a great way to improve your painting skills. Not only does a workshop allow you to concentrate on your painting without distractions, you also get the benefit of firsthand instruction while learning tried-and-true painting tips from an expert.

CHOOSING A WORKSHOP

Whether you attend local classes or travel to an artist's studio for a week-long workshop, there are a number of things you should consider when choosing and preparing for a painting seminar. It's always a good idea to call the instructor to find out what the workshop entails and what level of skill is required.

Many artists like to spend extra money to attend a week-long workshop in a fun location. If you can afford it, this is a good option as it allows time for personal contact with the instructor as well as the time to concentrate on and learn a new painting style.

With so many workshops available, you're sure to find one to fit all your needs. Consider the following:

• Location
• Accommodations (Are discount room rates offered for workshop attendees?)
• Transportation
• Cost
• Skill level of artists for whom the workshop is intended
• Medium used for workshop (Is it inexpensive? Is it good for beginners?)
• Class size
• Class length and pace (Is it intense or relaxed?)

A Recommended List of Supplies

paints
brushes
palette (or palette paper)
water (or turp) containers
lint-free paper towels
pencils
kneaded eraser
artist's tape
scissors
painting knife
stylus

tracing paper
transfer paper (gray and white)
chalk pencil
extender
brush cleaner
sandpaper
matte acrylic spray
ruler
paper

Handy Extras

blow dryer
magnifying glass
reducing glass
old toothbrush
cotton swabs and alcohol
facial tissue
finishing supplies (steel wool, soft cloth, varnish)
compass with pencil

sketchbook
folding stool (for any outdoor painting)
small folding luggage cart
camera
first aid kit
alarm clock
snacks

PACKING FOR YOUR WORKSHOP

The supply lists on page 118 include the basic materials you'll need for a painting seminar, as well as some extras you may find useful if you have the room. In most cases, the workshop instructor will provide you with a specific supply list. If this is the case, be sure to bring every item listed, and don't substitute products. Something you think will work may in fact be incompatible with the project the instructor has planned.

Consider the weather when choosing clothes for a workshop, as well as your own nature. (Are you normally too cold in an air-conditioned room?) Even if meals are provided, you may want to pack a few snacks if you normally get hungry between meals. If you're a smoker, be prepared not to smoke during a painting class—you should never smoke around flammable painting mediums, nor is it considerate of nonsmokers in the room.

GETTING THE MOST OUT OF YOUR WORKSHOP

Once you arrive at the workshop, be serious about what you're doing. Concentrate. Be on time. One of the biggest keys to success is putting

What to Expect

A typical first day at a painting seminar will begin with introductions to get everyone acquainted and relaxed. Next, the instructor will pass out any furnished supplies (surfaces, patterns and relevant instructions). Students will set up their materials and clear their areas of any unnecessary equipment.

The teacher will then explain the goal of the first project and launch right into the painting instruction. Although teaching styles will vary, the goal rarely does: for students to learn as much as possible in the time given.

A typical day may start at 9:00 A.M., with a brief mid-morning break. The agenda may include a critique of the previous day's work, or the instructor may jump right into a new project. There may be one more short break in the afternoon, and class will usually end around 5:00 P.M., with homework assignments often given for the next day's class.

aside what you think you know and listening to the instructor. Having an open mind and trying new techniques—no matter how skeptical you are—can be very rewarding in the end, even if you find out that the technique doesn't work for you. Try to relax and trust the instructor's plan.

Most importantly, don't be intimidated. No one will expect you to be a master decorative artist; if you knew everything there was to know about decorative painting, you wouldn't need to attend a workshop. Learn all you can, and have fun!

RESOURCES

A list of resources for the decorative painter is below. It includes advice on everything from the newest pattern packets to a list of workshops in your area.

DECORATIVE PAINTING BOOKS

As decorative painting continues to gain popularity, you're sure to see more high-quality, full color instructional and inspirational decorative painting books on the market. Check local and chain bookstores in the craft, hobby, home decorating and art sections.

In addition, most craft and hobby stores carry a selection of less expensive paperback booklets containing several projects each. These are usually located in the art instruction section.

A third option is to join Decorative Artist's Book Club, which was launched in January, 1997. This book club allows you to choose from a wide range of books specifically for decorative painters. For information on joining the club, contact Jim Walding, 1507 Dana Avenue, Cincinnati, OH 45207.

PATTERN PACKETS

Many well-known decorative artists and crafters publish and sell pattern packets. These packets typically contain complete instructions for one project—including a materials list, color chart, step-by-step instructions for painting the piece and a full-size pattern of the design. You'll find these packets in abundance at decorative painting and craft conventions, where you can stroll down the aisles and check out the finished products, then purchase instructions to recreate any project that strikes your fancy.

If you can't get to a convention, check out the advertising section of any of the decorative painting magazines on the market, such as *Decorative Artist's Workbook*, for mail-order patterns. Some craft and hobby stores also carry these packets.

LOCAL CLASSES

Be sure to check the bulletin boards and events schedules at your local museum, art center, craft store, community college, YMCA or other community center for decorative painting classes. Many are often offered at night or on the weekends.

CONVENTION AND WORKSHOP INFORMATION

Many decorative painting conventions and shows are held annually throughout the country, including national shows such as the Society of Decorative Painters National Convention and regional shows such as the Heart of Ohio Tole Convention held in Columbus, Ohio

In addition, many well-known artists teach seminars around the country or offer week-long workshops in their own studios. To keep up-to-date on national conventions, seminars and workshop dates, your best references are decorative painting magazines and craft store and decorative painting society newsletters.

THE SOCIETY OF DECORATIVE PAINTERS

The Society of Decorative Painters (SDP) was founded in 1972 as a volunteer membership organization. Its members are decorative painters from across the United States, Canada and 34 foreign countries. It has 243 affiliated chapters that actively promote the art form through community service projects and other painting-related activities.

The purpose of the Society is "to act as a central dissemination point for information about activities related to decorative painting; raise and maintain a high standard for the art of decorative painting; and stimulate interest in and appreciation for the art form."

The Society publishes *The Decorative Painter*, a bimonthly magazine for members. The Society hosts an annual national convention and has also assembled the world's largest collection of decorative painting pieces. For membership information, contact the Society's national office at 393 North McLean Blvd., Wichita, KS 67203. Tel: (316) 269-9300.

Credits

The publisher would like to give credit and many thanks to the artists, photographers and contributors who generously allowed their work to be reprinted in this book.

Pages 8–9, and line drawing on page 120, by Debra L. Welty.

Page 10, strokework wooden box and tin canister by Phillip C. Myer. Sunflower mailbox by Peggy Nuttall, author of *An Old-Fashioned Garden*, vols. I and II, a Gretchen Cagle Publication. Porcelain rose jar by Aileen Bratton, 9000 Caminito Dr. NE, Albuquerque, NM 87111, (505) 822-1965. Photography by BKT Photography.

Pages 12-21, by Joyce Morrison; demos by Gayle Laible.

Page 13, brush photo by Ron Forth Photography.

Pages 15 and 18, additional tips by Jackie Shaw.

Pages 22 and 27, photos by Ron Forth Photography.

Pages 22-27, by Phillip C. Myer.

Pages 28-31, by Joyce Morrison; photos by Ron Forth Photography.

Pages 32-33, by Jackie Shaw.

Page 34, by Phillip C. Myer (top left); Jackie Shaw (center, bottom); and Andy B. Jones (top right).

Page 35, by Jackie Shaw and Andy B. Jones (bottom); photo by Ron Forth Photography (bottom).

Page 36, by Priscilla Hauser; photo by BKT Photography.

Page 37, by Phillip C. Myer.

Page 38, by Priscilla Hauser.

Page 39, by Priscilla Hauser; photo by BKT Photography.

Page 40, by Priscilla Hauser; photo by Ron Forth Photography.

Page 41, by Dorothy Egan; photo by BKT Photography.

Page 42, by Sandra Buckingham.

Page 43, by Phillip C. Myer.

Pages 44-45, by Phillip C. Myer; silk painting by Marjorie Beck; photo by Ron Forth Photography.

Page 46, by Priscilla Hauser.

Page 47, by David Pyle; "Wetting Your Paper" and "Stretching Your Paper" by Zoltan Szabo; photo by Pam Monfort.

Page 48, by Priscilla Hauser.

Page 49, by Ginger Edwards; photo by Ron Forth Photography.

Page 50, by Millie Wurdeman.

Page 51, by Pat Olson.

Page 52, by Phillip C. Myer.

Page 53, by Phillip C. Myer; tip box by Priscilla Hauser.

Page 54, by Phillip C. Myer.

Page 55, by Andy B. Jones; photo by Ron Forth Photography.

Page 56, by Phillip C. Myer; tip box by Priscilla Hauser; illustration by Gretchen Cagle.

Page 57, by Phillip C. Myer; tip box by Gretchen Cagle.

Page 58, by Sherry Nelson; apples by Linda Wise; apple photo by Ron Forth Photography.

Page 59, demos by Gayle Laible.

Page 60, by Phillip C. Myer.

Page 61, by Susan Scheewe; demos by Gayle Laible.

Page 62, by Phillip C. Myer.

Page 63, demos by Gayle Laible.

Pages 64-65, by Phillip C. Myer; stenciling tips by Jane Gauss.

Pages 66-71, by Phillip C. Myer.

Page 71, *strié* photos from *Creative Paint Finishes for the Home*, copyright © 1992 by Phillip Myer. Used with permission of North Light Books. Photography by Russell Brannon Photography.

Pages 72-73, by Doxie Keller; finger rouging project by Phillip C. Myer.

Page 74, from *Creative Paint Finishes for Furniture*, copyright © 1996 by Phillip Myer. Used with permission of North Light Books. Photography by Michael LaRiche.

Page 75, by Sharon Buononato.

Pages 76-79, by Phillip C. Myer.

Pages 80 and 82, illustrations by Patrick Kelley Browne.

Pages 81 and 83, illustrations by Julie Baker.

Pages 85-87, by Betty L. Byrd.

Pages 88-89, by Bobbie Pearcy.

Page 94, photography by BKT Photography.

Page 99, by David Pyle.

Pages 100-105, by Jackie Shaw and Victoria Stone.

Pages 118-119, by Sherry Nelson and Anne Hevener.

Page 120, photography by BKT Photography.

Source listings compiled by Anne Hevener.

INDEX

More Great Books for Great Crafts!

Acrylic Decorative Painting Techniques—Discover stroke-by-stroke instruction for 50 fun and easy decorative painting techniques. Then you'll develop your own style as you explore various tools, materials, color, preparation and backgrounds. *#30884/$24.99/128 pages/550 color illus.*

Painting & Decorating Birdhouses—These 22 colorful easy-to-do decorative painting projects are for the birds! Learn how to transform unfinished birdhouses into something special—from a quaint Victorian roost to a rustic log cabin. *#30882/$23.99/128 pages/194 color illus.*

Making Books by Hand—Discover 12 beautiful and versatile projects for making handmade photo albums, scrapbooks, journals and more. Only everyday items like cardboard, wrapping paper, glue and ribbon are required. *#30942/$24.99/108 pages/250 color illus.*

Painting Greeting Cards in Watercolor—Create delicate, transparent colors and exquisite detail in these 35 fun and easy watercolor projects. Use them for greeting cards, framed art, postcards, gifts and more. *#30871/$22.99/128 pages/349 color illus.*

Decorative Painting with Gretchen Cagle—Discover decorative painting at its finest as you browse through pages of charming motifs. You'll brighten walls, give life to old furniture, create unique accent pieces and special gifts using step-by-step instructions, traceable drawings, detailed color mixes and more! *#30803/$24.99/144 pages/64 color, 36 b&w illus./paperback*

Creative Paint Finishes for Furniture—Revive your furniture with fresh color and design! Inexpensive, easy and fun painting techniques are at your fingertips, along with step-by-step directions and a photo gallery of imaginative applications for faux finishing, staining, stenciling, mosaic, découpage and many other techniques. *#30748/$27.99/144 pages/236 color, 7 b&w illus.*

Creative Paint Finishes for the Home—A complete, full-color step-by-step guide to decorating floors, walls and furniture— including how to use the tools, master the techniques and develop ideas. *#30426/$27.99/144 pages/212 color illus.*

Painting Houses, Cottages and Towns on Rocks—Discover how a dash of paint can turn humble stones into charming cottages, churches, Victorian mansions, and more. This hands-on, easy-to-follow book offers a menagerie of fun—and potentially profit-

able—stone animal projects. Eleven examples, complete with material list, photos of the finished piece and patterns will help you create entire rock villages. *#30823/$21.99/128 pages/398 color illus./paperback*

Creative Silk Painting—Uncover the secrets of silk painting as you get the inside story on how to apply brilliant color to silk and create beautiful art more quickly and easily. You'll explore exciting new topics, including new instant set dyes, creative painting techniques, creating garments and textile art and much more! *#30713/$26.99/144 pages/120 color illus.*

Stencil Source Book 2—Add color and excitement to fabrics, furniture, walls and more with over 200 original motifs that can be used again and again! Idea-packed chapters will help you create dramatic color schemes and themes to enhance your home in hundreds of ways. *#30730/$22.99/144 pages/300 illus.*

Master Works: How to Use Paint Finishes to Transform Your Surroundings—Discover how to use creative paint finishes to enhance and excite the "total look" of your home. This step-by-step guide contains dozens of exciting ideas on fresco, marbling, paneling and other simple paint techniques for bringing new life to any space. Plus, you'll also find innovative uses for fabrics, screens and blinds. *#30626/$29.95/176 pages/150 color illus.*

Create Your Own Greeting Cards and Gift Wrap with Priscilla Hauser—You'll see sponge prints, eraser prints, cellophane scrunching, marbleizing, paper making and dozens of other techniques you can use to make unique greetings for all your loved ones. *#30621/$24.99/128 pages/230 color illus.*

The Crafts Supply Sourcebook—Turn here to find the materials you need—from specialty tools and the hardest-to-find accessories, to clays, doll parts, patterns, quilting machines and hundreds of other items! Listings organized by area of interest make it quick and easy! *#70344/$18.99/320 pages/paperback*

Paint Craft—Discover great ideas for enhancing your home, wardrobe and personal items. You'll see how to master the basics of mixing and planning colors, how to print with screen and linoleum to create your own stationery, how to enhance old glassware and pottery pieces with unique patterns and motifs and much more! *#30678/$16.99/144 pages/200 color illus./paperback*

Nature Craft—Dozens of step-by-step nature craft projects to create, including dried flower garlands, baskets, corn dollies, potpourri and more. Bring the outdoors inside with these wonderful projects crafted with readily available natural materials. *#30531/$16.99/144 pages/200 color illus./paperback*

Paper Craft—Dozens of step-by-step paper craft projects to make, including greeting cards, boxes and desk sets, jewelry and pleated paper blinds. If you have ever worked with or wanted to work with paper you'll enjoy these attractive, fun-to-make projects. *#30530/$16.95/144 pages/200 color illus./paperback*

The Complete Book of Silk Painting—Create fabulous fabric art—everything from clothing to pillows to wall hangings. You'll learn every aspect of silk painting in this step-by-step guide, including setting up a workspace, necessary materials and fabrics and specific silk painting techniques. *#30362/$26.99/128 pages/4-color throughout*

Jewelry & Accessories: Beautiful Designs to Make and Wear—Discover how to make unique jewelry out of papier mache, wood, leather, cloth and metals. You'll learn how to create: a hand-painted wooden brooch, a silk-painted hair slide, a paper and copper necklace and much more! Fully illustrated with step-by-step instructions. *#30680/$17.99/128 pages/150 color illus./paperback*

Decorative Boxes To Create, Give and Keep—Craft beautiful boxes using techniques including embroidery, stenciling, lacquering, gilding, shellwork, decoupage and many other. Step-by-step instructions and photographs detail every project. *#30638/$15.95/128 pages/4-color throughout/paperback*

Everything You Ever Wanted to Know About Fabric Painting— Discover how to create beautiful fabrics! You'll learn how to set up work space, choose materials, plus the ins and outs of tie-dye, screen printing, woodgraining, marbling, cyanotype and more! *#30625/$21.99/128 pages/4-color throughout/paperback*

Painting Murals—Learn through eight step-by-step projects how to choose a subject for a mural, select colors that will create the desired effects and transfer the design to the final surface. *#30081/$29.99/168 pages/125 color illus.*

Holiday Fun Year-Round with Dian Thomas—Discover how to turn mere holiday observances into opportunities to exercise imagination and turn the festivity all the way up. You'll find suggestions for a memorable New Year's celebration, silly April Fool's Day pranks, recipes and ideas for a Labor Day family get-together, creative Christmas giving and much more! *#70300/$19.99/144 pages/150 color illus./ paperback*

Painting Baby Animals with Peggy Harris—Now you can paint adorable baby animals with the help of professional oil painter Peggy Harris! You'll learn her fun, exciting and virtually foolproof method of painting using 11 color, step-by step projects that show you how to paint a variety of realistic little critters—from puppies and kittens to ducklings and fawns. *#30824/$21.99/128 pages/319 color illus./ paperback*

The North Light Artist's Guide to Materials & Techniques—Shop smart with this authoritative guide to buying and using art materials in today's most popular mediums—from watercolor, oil and acrylic to charcoal, egg tempera and mixed media. You'll find personal recommendations and advice from some of North Light's most popular artists, as well as informed discussions on basic techniques, shopping lists, paints, surfaces, brushes and more! *#30813/ $29.99/192 pages/230+ color illus.*

Capturing the Magic of Children in Your Paintings—Create fresh, informal portraits that express the lively spirit and distinct personalities of children! In this book, designed to help artists in all the popular mediums, Jessica Zemsky shares the lessons she's learned in her many years of painting children—from finding natural poses to rendering varied skin and hair textures. *#30766/$27.99/128 pages/130+ color illus.*

How to Capture Movement in Your Paintings—Add energy and excitement to your paintings with this valuable guide to the techniques you can use to give your artwork a sense of motion. Using helpful, step-by-step exercises, you'll master techniques such as dynamic composition and directional brushwork to convey movement in human, animal and landscape subjects. *#30811/$27.99/144 pages/350+ color illus.*

Wildlife Painting Step By Step—Discover how to turn oils, watercolors, acrylics or pastels into creatures with fur, feathers or scales! Patrick Seslar and 13 distinguished wildlife artists reveal their complete painting process from developing the idea to adding final details. *#30708/$28.99/144 pages/195 color illus.*

100 Keys to Great Calligraphy—Lift your calligraphy out of the ordinary and turn it into something striking and original! You'll learn how to select suitable pens, inks and paper; achieve better pen control; plan a layout; and introduce color into your work. *#30819/$17.99/64 pages/150 color illus.*

Handmade Jewelry: Simple Steps to Creating Wearable Art—Create unique and wearable pieces of art—and have fun doing it! 42 step-by-step jewelry-making projects are at your fingertips—from necklaces and earrings, to pins and barrettes. Plus, no experience, no fancy equipment and no expensive materials are required! *#30820/ $21.99/128 pages/126 color, 30 b&w illus./ paperback*

Creating Textures in Colored Pencil—Add new dimension to your colored pencil work with these techniques for creating a rich variety of texture effects. More than 55 lifelike textures are covered, using clear, step-by-step demos and easy-to-do techniques, plus special tricks for getting that "just right" look! *#30775/$27.99/128 pages/175 color illus.*

Creating Textures in Pen & Ink with Watercolor—Create exciting texturing effects—from moss to metal to animal hair—with these step-by-step demonstrations from renowned artist/instructor Claudia Nice. *#30712/$27.99/144 pages/120 color, 10 b&w illus.*

Decorative Stencils for Your Home—Here are 20 stenciling projects to add interest and color to furniture, floors, walls and curtains—in any style of home. *#30843/$27.99/128 pages/250 illus.*

Fake Your Own Antiques—Transform junk-shop finds and ordinary furniture into eye-catching "antiques." With over 40 step-by-step projects. *#30841/$24.99/128 pages/200+ color illus*

100 Keys to Great Fabric Painting—Get 100 simple gems of advice from experienced fabric painters that will help you achieve professional results. *#30822/$17.99/64 pages/130 color illus.*

Making & Decorating Picture Frames—Create picture-perfect frames with these 45 imaginative and original projects using a variety of techniques and materials. *#30807/$24.99/128 pages/250+ color illus.*

The Best of Pottery—Here's the first international collection to honor the beautiful, time-honored art of pottery. Over 200 works featured! *#30863/$24.99/144 pages/ 250+ color illus.*

Paper Sculpture—See how 9 award-winning paper sculptors transform paper into exciting 3-D sculptures. *#30853/$22.99/ 152 pages/300 color illus/paperback*